A
Naturalist's
Field
Guide

A
Naturalist's
Field
Guide

Lawrence Kilham

Stackpole Books

Published by
STACKPOLE BOOKS
Cameron and Kelker Streets
P.O. Box 1831
Harrisburg, Pa. 17105

Published simultaneously in Don Mills, Ontario, Canada by
Thomas Nelson & Sons, Ltd.

Jacket photograph courtesy of Chuck Hummer

Printed in the U.S.A.

Library of Congress Cataloging in Publication Data

Kilham, Lawrence, 1910–
  A naturalist's field guide.

  Bibliography: p.
  1. Natural history—Addresses, essays, lectures.
2. Birds—Addresses, essays, lectures. 3. Outdoor life—
Addresses, essays, lectures. I. Title.
QH81.K538   1981   591   81-8882
ISBN 0-8117-1012-2   AACR2

PREFACE

I owe a great deal to my brother Peter Kilham, president of Droll Yankees Incorporated, who first suggested the idea of writing the book and who has given it every encouragement. Much is owed also to my wife, Jane, who not only made most of the illustrations, but has aided my bird studies for years in innumerable ways, ranging from rearing nestling birds to aid in finding and watching at nests. A few of the illustrations were made by my daughter Phoebe. The book is thus something of a family affair, with a cover contributed by my niece, Anne Kilham.

Others who helped in completing the book were Steve Libby, who read the manuscript, and Mrs. Dorothy Wallace who did the typing.

Many of the chapters have appeared as articles in Audubon and other journals and I much appreciate the permission of the editors to use them or portions of them here. These acknowledgements are to the *Bulletin of the Massachusetts Audubon Society* for "Fox Cubs by the Bear Camp" (December, 1947) and "A Porcupine that Needed Attention" (October, 1949); to the *Atlantic Naturalist* for "The Island of Barro Colorado" (November-December, 1950); "Beaver and Wildlife" (May-August, 1951); "Small Mammals from Earthy Runways" (November-December, 1951); "Owls in the Library" (January-February, 1954); "The Delinquent Crows" (March-April, 1953); and "Watching Mammals" (January-February, 1954); To the *New Hampshire Audubon Quarterly* for "Tree Den of Fisher"

(Winter, 1970); "Cabin in the South" (Fall, 1973); "June on a Maine Island" (Summer, 1974); "Birds of a Hemlock Cone Year" (Fall, 1975) and "Kingfishers in the Garden" (Fall, 1976). Acknowledgement is due to *The Animal Kingdom Magazine* of the New York Zoological Society for the chapter on hornbills (March-April, 1958). I would also like to thank Mr. Frederick Winthrop for letting my wife and I study woodpeckers on the Groton Plantation, Luray, South Carolina.

Throughout the book I have followed the convention used by ornithological journals of capitalizing names such as Downy Woodpecker and Red-breasted Nuthatch that refer to individual species, and using small letters for such terms as woodpeckers and nuthatches that, when used alone, are collective terms.

Lawrence Kilham
Lyme, N.H.

CONTENTS

viii

I. CABIN IN THE SOUTH

". . . as the days went slowly by we came to live for the moment, taking limitless pleasure in the small adventures that came our way." - - - G. B. Schaller.

Jane and I headed south from New Hampshire in our four-wheel-drive Travelall in mid-March, having no idea where we might stay. We were prepared to camp out. I had an invitation to study woodpeckers on a 23-thousand acre plantation along the Savannah River, but the idea of staying at a motel and having to commute was far from pleasing. We arrived at the plantation, therefore, with uncertainties. These cleared when the manager asked if we would like to camp in a cabin used by himself and friends for hunting in the fall.

The little white-washed cabin turned out to be ideal. We had brought the needed equipment and, moving in, made ourselves at home at the edge of a cypress swamp two miles in depth and bordering the river. The swamp, hung with masses of Spanish moss, was endlessly fascinating. Not the least of its fascinations were flood waters that lapped at the steps of our veranda.

Nature came to us in various ways. By the middle of the afternoon we began to hear a chorus of Barred Owls that was to make the swamp resound through the night. In New Hampshire I had never encountered these birds in more than single pairs, but here they seemed to have divided the swamp into innumerable territories. The owls were highly vocal, communicating with each other in a mixture of hootings and caterwaulings that were the more eerie coming through isles of Spanish moss.

The owls were not the only noisemakers. Pileated Woodpeckers, like the owls, were more abundant than in New England. There were three pairs along the stretch of swamp by the cabin and their loud "cuk, cuks" and rolling drums made the swamp still further alive. Individual Pileateds made a stream of "cuks" as they flew to roost holes at sunset.

As the Pileated Woodpeckers became silent, Jane and I became aware that Red-headed Woodpeckers were among the last of the local birds to retire. They lived on small, winter-type territories along the swamp and raised a commotion of "quirrs' and rattles, at rates of up to 72 per minute, as dusk approached. But when flying to their roost holes they became silent. One next to the cabin flew so fast to his sleeping place that I could easily have missed him had not the "white shirttails" of his lower wings revealed his whereabouts.

By the time stars were out and the owls at their peak, we were in our bunks for a night's sleep preparatory to arising at dawn. It was then we discovered that we were sharing the cabin with another occupant. This was Ratty. Although Ratty had a scaly tail and the dimensions of an ordinary rat, she was actually a wood or pack rat (*Neotoma floridana*), living much as deer mice live in cabins in New Hampshire.

Ratty was noisy at night. We believed she was a prospective mother preparing a nest for she found much in the way of pans and other objects that needed rearranging under the sink. If I got up to pound the walls, hoping she she would stop, she would cease one racket and begin another—a steady "thump, thump, thump". I imagined she made it by stamping her hind feet on some resounding board as a way of expressing annoyance. But in his book on mammals Cahalane says wood rats make the noise by vibrating the terminal third of their tails.

One might ask why we did not set a trap and have the cabin to ourselves. But Jane and I had met Ratty face to face. The large peaceful eyes that looked at us dispelled any thought of using a trap. I sought, instead, to block up all holes that I could find.

Nothing, however, stopped Ratty for long. What she wanted was stuffing from a mattress at the end of the cabin and she generally found ways of unplugging one hole or another to accomplish her purpose. Except for the mattress, she left other things pretty much alone. A single exception was the night we left a loaf of bread on the table. By morning Ratty had taken all of it, slice by slice, to her home among the pots and pans.

* * * * * * * * *

Cardinals and the cooings of Mourning Doves greeted us when we stepped from the cabin at dawn. Wherever we walked, the predominant and most striking birds were woodpeckers. Of these, the Red-bellied and Red-headeds were the most numerous, followed by flickers, Downies and finally Red-cockadeds. In our first days I spent much time locating colonies of these latter birds—not as difficult as it might seem for, as is well known, they excavate holes in living pines all in one area.

Red-cockadeds make gashes in the sapwood of their pines that stimulate pitch to flow above and below their holes. I soon found that although the Red-cockadeds made the holes, nearly half of them were occupied by intruders. Red-bellieds and Red-headeds were the most numerous. Other holes had occupants as varied as flying squirrels and White-breasted Nuthatches.

A tragedy over much of the South is that although the actual nest trees of Red-cockaded Woodpeckers have often been spared, the lumbering of mature pines in the neighborhood has left the woodpeckers without places to dig new holes, once the old ones have become uninhabitable or occupied by competitors.

* * * * * * * * * *

After a morning of roaming about the plantation I was ready to sit on the cabin porch, writing notes and gazing out into the sunlit swamp. It was not difficult to spend one or two hours in this way. There was always something to watch.

I liked to scan old logs for snakes or turtles. On one I saw what I first thought was a piece of woody vine. It turned out to be the triangular head of a cotton-mouth. The snake had its head raised and, as I watched, it slid into the water and swam toward the veranda. I thought, "how enormous, six feet long, two inches thick, and coming so close!"

In my excitement I had forgotten I was watching through field glasses! When I glanced down without them, I saw that the moccasin was actually only a little over three feet long. It rested on a root just below the cabin flicking his tongue at us. Here was nature, flooding to the doorstep!

The sunlit swamp, with its cypresses, tupelos, sweet gum and other trees just coming into leaf, had many beautiful sights. An occasional Great Egret, flying among the tree trunks with white plumage resplendent in the sun, was among the most striking. What I searched for was the Yellow-throated Warbler.

I suppose all who watch birds have their favorites. Yellow-throateds have long been one of mine because, as warblers go, they are relatively large and slow-moving. This allows one to follow them as they poke about and cling to clumps of Spanish moss. Their plumage, of extreme beauty, is worn by male and female alike. They are a bird of two habitats. Sometimes I found them in nearby loblolly pines pushing their way among clusters of needles in a manner not unlike their associates, the Pine Warblers. In the swamp, on the other hand, they shared the Spanish moss with Parula Warblers, both species using it for nesting.

Some creatures came to the veranda. Jane had set a coffee can under the eaves and a Carolina Wren busied itself by filling it with nest material. A quick-eyed anole came to the porch also. Anole is, of course, the correct name for chameleons sold at circuses.

* * * * * * * * *

As days passed I came to spend much time at the colonies of Red-cockaded Woodpeckers because wherever located, they seemed to be a focal point for a variety of other hole-nesters. At one colony I heard the sound of steady excavating and traced it to a hole at the top of a pine stub where a Pileated Woodpecker had nearly finished its nest hole. In weeks that followed I spent hours watching the nesting of these magnificent birds.

I had much else to watch. In a small stub near that of the Pileateds a pair of Brown-headed Nuthatches—those attractive midgets—carried on courtship by a hole in a dead pine that was also attracting a pair of Downy Woodpeckers. Nor were these the only goings-on that kept my field glasses moving.

Jane and I usually sat close to a living pine where a pair of Red-bellied Woodpeckers were appropriating a roost/nest cavity made by Red-cockadeds, undeterred by the mass of pitch around the entrance. Red-cockadeds keep pitch flowing by working daily on their gashes.

To my surprise I found one of them working on the gashes of the tree taken over by the Red-bellieds. It seemed strange that the Red-cockaded should have continued to work on a pine no longer its own. The gashes are made to promote a flow of pitch that is presumed to protect against tree-climbing snakes.

* * * * * * * * * *

The plantation by the Savannah River was a woodpecker paradise. It was also a quail management area and this gave us much to think about.

There can be little doubt that man has a strong hunting instinct. Finding birds, then sitting down to watch them, is one way of satisfying this urge—at least for a small number of naturalists. The bird-watcher needs no equipment other than a pair of field glasses. But Jane and I also carry lightweight aluminum chairs so that we may sit comfortably wherever we may be.

After our three-weeks experience in South Carolina we would add just one more item of equipment to this kind of nature-watching: a small cabin in which to live. By so doing, one may enjoy the changes of dawn, midday, sunset and the night—even if one has to spend so much of the latter trying to outsmart a wood rat about to have young.

II. NATURE AT THE CENTER OF THINGS

"With Laotse and Chuangtse, on the other hand, nature was constantly at the center of their thinking. Man divorced from nature, they argued, could not be happy; and man's power to resist nature was hopelessly puny." Yukawa.

I sat in our cabin writing my notes surrounded by sun-patched woodland that I saw from our window. The pull of the out-of-doors on this April day was strong. Every few minutes I stepped to the veranda to look out over the flood waters of the Savannah River that came nearly to the steps. There was something vibrant, alive, exciting about this southern swamp . . . the bright green sprays of cypress; the delicate grey of Spanish moss; a male Parula Warbler with his handsome pattern of yellow below, bluish on head and wings, and green patch on back, flying after small insects just over the water.

When days were hot along open, sandy roads, it was contrastingly cool by the swamp. Everything was restful, quietly beautiful. There was always something to catch the eye. A bright-eyed anole turned its sharp little snout to scan leaves close to the porch. A Cardinal gathered strands from a clump of Spanish moss to build a nest. A Summer Tanager in plumage of tropical brilliance moved slowly from limb to limb.

Jane and I sat on the veranda turning our glasses to one thing and then another. In this, our second year at the cabin, we saw many of the same things as before. Yet to live surrounded by nature was what we loved. A Carolina Wren was coming to add sticks to the old coffee can we had set up under the eaves. His industry reminded me that I should be back in the cabin writing my journal. Was not my journal somewhat the same—a place to accumulate sticks and twigs of observations collected in various places?

Would the Carolina wren ever use his nest, seemingly one of several he was building at the same time? The thought did not seem to bother him. He worked *"con mucho gusto"*, as the Spanish say—for the love of it. I felt the same way about my journal.

* * * * * * * * * *

I was in the cabin again in the early afternoon when I heard a stir outside. Was it Jane coming down the path? No, she was on the veranda. I peered out the window and caught a glimpse of a Wood Duck. By the time I reached the path the duck was waddling straight toward me making steady "K-duck, K-duck" notes to five tiny ducklings, their black heads and mottled yellow bodies soft and downy in the sunlight. They followed their mother in a tight huddle as she led them toward me and the water. Ten feet away she made a detour, reaching the swamp in safety.

One duckling lagged behind and the mother turned to wait. Then they all swam away among the tree trunks of the flood waters.

What a satisfying spectacle of how much in nature works with wondrous efficiency! The ducklings obeyed while the mother lead them past danger—the mother with one set of instincts, the ducklings with another . . . and the two sets meshing perfectly. I wondered if, when I first heard the mother, the ducklings had not just come from a nest in the stub of a dead oak standing in a clearing above the path.

* * * * * * * * * *

What peace, what quiet was ours! How closely nature came about us. Common place things like Cardinals and anoles became of entrancing interest when one was relaxed and at peace. "Only the healthiest man in the world," wrote Thoreau, "is sensible to the finest influence—affected by more or less of electricity in the air."

As I stood on our porch another early afternoon a Wood Thrush came down onto damp ground left by receding waters. What an alert and vigorous bird! Through with one spot, a few hops on its longish legs carried it swiftly a dozen feet away to another. Then off the end of the porch I noticed a stir in low, tangled vegetation. It was our Carolina Wren, tail cocked up as it rustled in and out of a miniature jungle. Beyond the wren was a pair of Cardinals.

Then I saw something new, a most beautiful bird: a Painted Bunting fluttering at the tops of plants growing on the woodland floor. Occasional shafts of sunlight lit up its brilliant plumage.

How much nature has to offer if, looking for nothing, one takes what comes. A hummingbird flew toward me, stopping by a few flowers, then hovering ever-so-briefly before my eyes as if they might be something else to visit.

* * * * * * * * * *

I had brought a few books to read yet I felt how

superfluous they were. Man lived for eons of time without the printed word. Did not my books compete for the life of the senses when I was living in such a place as the edge of the swamp? This did not mean they were not welcome, and very much so, under the right circumstances. But in the cabin I threw "Zorba the Greek" away as a robber of my time.

"Take the fish without the net" is a Zen saying I love. The "fish" that I retained from Zorba lay in a few sentences. "He interrogates himself with the same amazement when he sees a man, a tree in bloom, a glass of cold water. Zorba sees every day as if for the first time."

* * * * * * * * * *

A west wind swept in from the pines as I walked along the sandy road late one afternoon. How Jane and I would miss this freedom, this leisure, this absence of chores to do when, back in New England, we faced another winter's imprisonment!

There was a flash of white in the sun as a Red-headed Woodpecker flew from a field, and headed straight through an open grove before gliding steeply upward to alight on the trunk of a pine. There it rested, scanning the ground for another insect to capture.

I now passed through the stubble of last year's cornfield to a tall, weathered dead pine. Another Red-headed Woodpecker—one of a pair Jane and I had been watching—perched near the top. With a flash of wings that made it look largely white, it beat its way toward the late afternoon sun to catch an insect. Then, with a long glide broken by a few wing beats, returned to its starting place.

"How to make the getting our living poetic," was Thoreau's thought. But all the birds I watched, were they not doing so every day—and in beautiful surroundings?

* * * * * * * * *

Another woodpecker we were following was the Red-bellied. When I was returning at the end of the day a male flew to a hole in a large dead pine—a hole originally carved by a Red-cockaded Woodpecker.

The rays of the sun, now low over the trees, shone on its bright red crown and nape. The faint red of its under-parts was in marked contrast to the handsome zebra bars on its back. It rested peacefully, giving occasional full-throated "kwirr, kwirrs." These at last brought his mate, who alighted before the hole as he departed. All he wanted was for her to come at his call, with assurance that she was still attached to him and their prospective nest.

How happy and content the lives of birds seem at times. Is this imaginary or is it something we see when we are happy and content?

It was while watching this same pair of woodpeckers a few evenings previously that Jane and I shared a remarkable experience—one of the more memorable we had in the southland. An incredible downpour at noon had made us feel as though the cabin was a boat and that it would soon float away. It might well have, for the flood waters of the Savannah River were already high.

The deluge stopped an hour later. All nature seemed to awaken with new life. In the charred, burnt-over land above the cabin termites swarmed from old stumps and tree trunks in nuptial flights.

These in turn attracted a colorful assortment of warblers—Yellow-throated, Parula and Prairie, all flying down low where I could see them.

But it was in the evening when Jane and I stopped to visit the pair of Red-bellied Woodpeckers that we experienced the full effects of the downpour. There was an incredible din arising in all directions from what must have been thousands of frogs of many species.

Mixed in with this symphony was a chorus of bullfrogs and a strange noise sounding like a flock of geese coming in low with a cacaphony of honks. I would have given a good deal to have learned what kind of frogs these latter were. To top it all Barred Owls joined in with hootings and Pileated Woodpeckers with "cuks", high calls, and drummings. Nothing Jane and I had heard before, even in Africa or Panama, rivalled the sheer volume of these voices of the downpour. What an evening to remember.

Remarkably enough, the following evening was a quiet one, with little singing of any kind.

* * * * * * * * * *

When twilight came we lit the lamps in the cabin and enjoyed its coziness. Looking at the rough boards and beams, it was strange to consider that this whitewashed shack had once been the kitchen of a slave family. It had only recently been hauled down alongside the swamp. Strange, also, to think that the fields we walked had once been tilled by slaves. But I am no sentimentalist. If many were happy, not all of the slaves were slaves any more than all so-called free men are free. "No man in the world is free," wrote Euripides, "slaves to all they own, or want, or fear." How many are really free in our competitive society?

What is the criterion of freedom? I think that it is to be able to give one's self to nature—to feel, as Thoreau said, "electricity in the air".

Thoughts of Thoreau and slavery brought to mind a story Thoreau tells in his journal. "There was wit and even poetry," said he, in the negro's answer to the man who tried to persuade him that the slaves would not be obliged to work in heaven. "Oh, you g'way, Massa, I know better. If der's no work for culled folks up dar, dey'll make some fur'em; and if der's nuffin better to do, dey'll make em shub de clouds along. You can't fool this chile, Massa."

A good thought for one about to turn in for the night: "shub de clouds along." I smiled and dropped off to sleep.

* * * * * * * * * *

It was the hour before dawn that I liked best. It was then that the experiences of the day before returned with the greatest clarity. And so I wrote while Jane prepared the bacon and grits.

"Nature is imagination itself," said William Blake. "As a man is, so he sees." If one can find unending interest in common things, with what enthusiasm can he look forward to each day's experience! Thus with the first streaks of dawn, I was prepared by a session of journal-writing, bacon and grits to go forth to my woodpeckers.

* * * * * * * * * *

Healthy, free, a morning of Red-headed and other woodpeckers before me. So I thought as I walked up the sandy road from the cabin, listening to a chorus of Mourning Doves, Mockingbirds and Cardinals as the last sounds of Barred Owls and Chuck-will's-widows faded into the coming dawn.

It was a cold morning with a new moon and one star still visible above the horizon. I needed winter clothing, hood and all, as I sat down before a dead pine with nest holes of both flicker and Red-headed Woodpecker. A mist rolled in over a plowed field. The female flicker clung quietly before her nest. I thought she was about to enter to lay another egg.

Mourning Doves, swift-flying and always in pairs, came to alight on the plowed fields as a Red-tailed Hawk circled over the plantation. Then I heard a soft "oik, oik" as a male flicker flew to the nest pine. His mate slipped into the hole but came out when he flew to a branch nearby. She followed and mating took place. Mating and egg-laying, as with all woodpeckers, go on thus in days of quiet courtship.

I later witnessed an odd incident. The flickers, frightened away by an inadvertent move on my part, had left the dead pine to the male Red-headed Woodpecker who was less easily frightened. After excavating his hole higher up, the Red-head rested in the sun, then dropped to the base of the pine. He now worked his way up, leisurely inspecting cracks and crevices.

On reaching the flicker's hole the Red-head bowed in to investigate several times before entering. What mischief might he do inside? After what seemed a long time (but was probably only three minutes) he came out and wiped his bill, as though he had been eating. Then he re-entered.

Eggs for breakfast? There was not much question when the male emerged with a punctured egg, its contents gleaming in the morning sun. He lodged it at the base of a branch. At that moment the male flicker returned. The Red-head attacked but the flicker defended the vicinity of its nest. Apparently no great harm was done for the flickers continued with their nesting on subsequent days.

The incident might never have happened had I not, by chance, kept the flickers from their nest. Had the flickers remained on guard the Red-head would, in all probability, never have had the chance to enter.

Our mornings went by,I watching at some nests, later taking over where Jane had watched others. We wanted to learn all we could of the lives of our woodpeckers during their peak of courtship. But one should never become too narrowly oriented. My recurring thought when in open air is to always put the beauty of nature first. That done, all else seems to fall into place.

* * * * * * * * * *

As we usually watched our woodpeckers while sitting out under the pines, I little expected that one of our most interesting observations would come while we were inside the cabin. But so it was. I was by the window writing late one afternoon when I heard the loud "cuks" of a Pileated. There was nothing unusual in this for these woodpeckers, quiet earlier in the afternoon, often made the swamp resound with their calls from 4:30 or so on. The "cuks" on that afternoon suddenly came close. I looked out to see a male fly to the base of a tree by the water's edge and then, with continued "cuks", alight on a pile of dirt. He had obviously been there before. He settled down in a depression like a hen on a nest, his body feathers fluffed out and his crest raised. He jabbed into the dirt with his bill, pausing to raise his head and look about.

When his mate called from the swamp he answered with a high call before continuing to thrust his bill into the mound. He flew away after four minutes, some dirt falling from his plumage.

When I inspected the mound all I found was damp clay. I could see holes where the Pileated had jabbed his bill, but there was no sign of ants or other insects that might have attracted him. What was he doing? Many birds such as Domestic Sparrows and Ruffed Grouse take dust baths, working dirt into their plumages. But the Pileated could not do this with this dampish clay that rounded into small pellets.

I have only two guesses as to the meaning of the dirt bath: one is that feather and skin parasites, become especially active as spring advances, and that the Pileated was seeking relief from irritation by contact with the cool wet earth. Another guess is that many animals and birds have a desire to eat earth at times.

I saw this particularly in Blue Jays that Jane and I raised indoors. When they had become several months old they fed avidly on earth. Who knows but that a certain amount of dirt may be required by the digestive tract, even for birds spending much of their time in trees?

The Pileated returned to his dirt pile on subsequent days. Exceedingly heavy rains, though, had turned the soil to mud and the Pileated flew away each time after a few trial jabs.

* * * * * * * * *

Our life on the plantation, centering on the cabin, gave us a chance to make daily discoveries. One comes to realize that nature is full of things to discover to those who are free, imaginative and open. The sight of these things brings joy to life while discoveries keep the senses refreshed.

"Creativity and Intuition", by the Japanese Nobel prize-winning physicist, Hideki Yukawa, was a book I read with interest at the plantation. Speaking of physics, Yukawa says, "the new fact that is discovered must not simply be new but must have importance." When I thought about what we observed on the plantation I wondered what is new? What is important? Almost nothing one sees or discovers is new in any world sense yet all that one really observes can be intensely new to the individual himself. This is the important thing. As Goethe pointed out we cannot inherit; we have to discover for ourselves.

With these thoughts in mind, I remembered another passage taken from "Zorba the Greek". "If only I could take a cloth and wipe out all I have learnt," wrote Zorba's companion, "all I've seen and heard, and go to Zorba's school and start the great, the real alphabet. What a different road I would choose. I should keep my five senses perfectly trained, and my whole body, too, so it would enjoy and understand."

I ask again is it worth bringing such books as Yukawa and Zorba along when one is living simply, surrounded by nature? Is not nature enough? Nature expressed by the effortless sailing of a Turkey Vulture above fields of sprouting corn, or by a white egret flying through the light and shade of the cypress swamp? Yes and no. Nature must include human nature.

In finding kinship in certain thoughts with Laotse, Chuangtse, Yukawa and even Zorba, I feel that there are unities between human minds, however separated in time and space. That is, if one puts nature at the center of things.

III. A GEORGIA SEA ISLAND

"By a world of marsh that borders a
world
                of sea.
Sinuous southward and sinuous
northward
          the shimmering band
Of the sand-beach fastens the fringe of
        the marsh to the folds of the
        land."—Sidney Lanier

How best approach this island of Sapelo off the
coast of Georgia?

We might start as loggerhead turtles do when coming to lay eggs on the outer beach. The miles of beach
are usually empty, for Sapelo is a wildlife reserve
where Jane and I stayed as guests of the University of
Georgia's Marine Institute.

It was a March day with Brown Pelicans flying high
to make spectacular plunges into the sea when we
passed through a stretch of sand dunes to the causeway across a salt marsh. An occasional Great Egret,
wings bright in the sun, flew over the brown marsh
grass. Crossing a tidal creek where diamond back ter-
rapins swam, we saw banks of oysters growing in
waters free of pollution.

The causeway lead on to a grove of live oaks. Streamers of Spanish moss swayed in the sea winds. As we stopped to adjust from the glare of the sun we saw camelias, a row of azaleas and, farther on, dogwood and wisteria in bloom. Beds of resurrection ferns, fresh from a rain, flourished on the curved trunks of live oaks. With memories of snow and mud left behind in New Hampshire we could scarcely believe such a paradise of south sea breezes, Cardinals and Mockingbirds existed.

The road became a gravel path leading to statues of Diana about a swimming pool and beyond to what I called the "Petit Palais", an architectural gem with a portico lined by Italian tiles. Here, in one wing, Jane and I stayed for some weeks. Special privilege? Not exactly, for the building—part of what was once a private estate—is owned by the Marine Institute.

* * * * * * * * * *

Thus began three weeks of nothing to do but wander about and discover. I had come to the island to study Pileated Woodpeckers, but it was not always possible to find them. There were opportunities to observe the life of the island in going from one place to another.

Starting at sunrise I strolled between a row of cabbage palms and azaleas. Skirting a pond where coot and Common Gallinule pattered across lily pads, I entered a grove of loblolly pines that looked promising for woodpeckers. As though with beginner's luck my steps took me to an opening in the center of the grove. An exceedingly tall dead pine stood here and, near its top, I heard a sound of excavating. Could I have found the nest of a Pileated this easily? I walked a distance away and sat down to watch. Soon a male peered from a hole 70 feet up, scanned the sky and started to toss out sawdust.

A walk I often took following watchings by the nest was along a sandy road covered with pine needles. It ran through a pleasant wood of mixed pine, hollies and other trees to a second causeway. Part way along was a pond surrounded by cattails. Approaching cautiously, I looked between bushes to see an assortment of coot, Common Gallinule, Gadwall, scaup, Hooded Mergansers, Pintail, Bufflehead and other ducks. Searching along the edges I found Little Blue as well as Louisiana Herons.

But these were not what I sought one warm day when I scanned the water for the projecting snout and eyes of a large alligator. I had an especially good view as the 'gator floated like a log, brownish jaws and dark back well exposed. It swam slowly out among the waterfowl—they did not seem concerned. When I continued on toward the sea a small alligator, two-and-a-half feet long, crossed in front of me as it scurried from the pond to a slough on the other side.

I was soon on the outer beach with sun shining on miles of unspoiled shore. Sand dunes with tall, yellow grasses lay on one side and on the other, blue ocean came in with low surf.

Jane had walked from the far causeway along the beach, so we now met and unfolded our chairs to enjoy the view and compare notes. She had scanned the sands for shells; angel wings, common slipper, calico scallop, channeled whelk, giant Atlantic cockle and others. Her main find was a huge, half-mummified loggerhead turtle lying on the upper beach where it had died the breeding season before. We now knew, at first hand, that there were sizeable alligators as well as turtles on the island.

Royal Terns fished offshore as we sat enjoying the wind and waves. The terns flapped steadily along about 30 feet over the water with bills pointed down. Every so often one hovered then plunged, sending up a two-foot column of spray. Many shore birds moved close to us. In the vanguard were Sanderling, their black legs moving like clockwork as they ran in the ebb of the surf, slowing for a few rapid jabs, then racing on. Dunlin fed with the Sanderling on the wavelet-covered sand. Their bills probed without letup until they took wing. They then moved with swift precision, only to bank, flutter a few beats and alight against the wind.

On some days we saw Ringed Plover working above the waves and hence nearer to us. A bit beyond, higher tides had left a belt of shells and other wrack from the sea that attracted Ruddy Turnstones. These strikingly plumaged birds took time to stand about on their short legs, inspecting and turning over objects for whatever prey might lurk beneath. The largest shore birds on the beach were the Willets, but they were not giving the cries that make them so attractive over the marshes later in the spring.

Our best walks were north along the beach at Cabreta separated from Sapelo by a tidal inlet. Sometimes as many as a dozen Marbled Godwits, magnificent brown and buff birds, fed with the Sanderling on wet portions of the beach. One godwit, plunging the length of its long, upturned bill deep into the sand, came up with a worm three inches long.

A Black-bellied Plover was the champion worm-puller. It caught a worm that seemed endless. Just as a Robin deals with a nightcrawler, so this chunky bird pulled with gentle persistence, coaxing the worm inch by inch—ten, 12 and finally what may have been more than 15 inches of it, a thick and substantial morsel, all subsequently consumed. These plover usually do little but stand around, running only a few steps now and then. I suppose, after such a meal, a plover can afford to rest in idleness.

* * * * * * * * * *

A feature of Sapelo is that one can study the birds of the land as well as those of the sea; using the time

of day, the weather and tides as guides to what may
prove most profitable. A stormy onshore wind put a
damper on birding by the shore on the 20th of
March. How put in my time to advantage? I recalled a
drainage ditch that I called "Many Stump Swamp"
running through the interior of the island. It was
protected from the wind. Why not traverse the
swamp on a search for woodpecker holes?

A long, arduous walk yielded nothing, not even a
Yellow-rumped Warbler. The swamp finally nar-
rowed where the ditch entered a pine wood and
where cat briars snagged at every turn. What a wild
goose chase! Would I never reach the road at the far
end of this tangle?

There is a saying of Laotse that "good fortune
brings misfortune and misfortune good fortune." It is
a line that I think of particularly in relation to looking
for woodpeckers. Searches for their nests can be long
and discouraging. It is almost psychic that in low
moments, when prospects have looked bleak, that I
have suddenly found what I was looking for. So was it
on this rainy day.

As the thoughts of Laotse struck me I saw a dead
pine with a hole. Could it be that of a Pileated Woodpecker? It had been obviously made by one but it was
dark and looked several years old. Deflated, I pushed
on, scanning the ground to avoid the briars. Then I
saw fresh wood chips. I now backed away for another
view and saw, from this different angle, a new hole
well below the old one. A male Pileated was looking
out, seemingly unperturbed. He soon withdrew, I
presumed to continue incubating.

How long would it be before the female returned to
do her share? Sometimes changeovers are several
hours apart. I might have a long wait but luck was
with me when I settled down to watch. Within five

minutes the female, just seen from the corner of my eye, came to a pine some distance away. I focused my glass on the hole, keeping as motionless as possible. A sky that had been overcast began to light up and as the female alighted by the hole a shaft of sunlight struck the dead pine.

What a beautiful bird! Her back and longish tail were black, her crest, set off by the black of her forehead, a brilliant scarlet and the broad stripes down the side of her neck a gleaming white. Thus she paused, calm and undisturbed. She poked her bill into the hole, then withdrew to one side as her mate, crest raised, slipped out and off. I could see the flash of white under his black wings as he disappeared among the pines. Now alone, the female bowed into the nest, the tip of her tail disappearing slowly as she settled down inside.

This swamp nest was somewhat distant. With much to do on the island, including watches by the nest of the first Pileateds I had found, I neglected the swamp pair for some days. Little happens, after all, when these birds are incubating. But just how long were the times between change-overs of male and female? I thought I had better find out.

Luck still held at the nest in the dead pine. I had hardly sat down, partially ensconced in honeysuckle, before the male flew in. He paused by the hole as his mate left. Then he entered. Noting the time I settled back for a long vigil. Would not the wait become boring and tiresome? How control my restlessness? The pine wood was essentially birdless. I had little to look at.

After a half hour had passed I found myself becoming less restless. I began to think how glorious it was to be simply "going nowhere, doing nothing."

Man's trouble is that he never gives his senses a chance. But here on this beautiful island, I now had a little world of my own: there was a gentle wind in the pines, vultures occasionally soared overhead, and patches of sunlight brightened the pine needles.

Who knows; perhaps the Pileated down in his nest hole saw something of the sky, and heard the wind in the pines just as I did.

Thus one hour and most of another passed. I was content, enjoying. These hours were, in retrospect, among the more memorable of those spent on the island.

After an hour and three-quarters, just about the time I had given up on the female returning, she was suddenly there! As before the male, swung out, crest raised, and flew off. She slipped in to take her turn as the two birds shared their task of incubating.

* * * * * * * * * *

March 27 was an unusually cold day, yet a glorious one to be out in the wind and sun. In the evening Jane and I took a walk along the causeway to the beach. An almost full moon was rising above the sand dunes ahead. Behind the sun was setting over the marsh with its maze of tidal creeks.

Tall yellow grasses of the dunes caught the last of the sun, as did curling breakers on the beach. There was more stir in the air than usual—more whiteness and spray as waves were whipped in an unusually high tide.

A solitary scaup rode the breakers, now down in a trough, now up on an incoming wave, bobbing lightly to the far side as a wave curled and broke. Ten Sanderling ran along the edge of the sea foam. They ran fast, with infrequent stops to probe. A few, flying fast outside the breakers, flashed the black and white of wings and backs in the last of the sun.

We turned to go. The sun had left the sea, but high up 20 or more gulls circled in its rays, much as swallows rise on summer evenings. We walked back along the causeway in the dusk to the cackling of Clapper Rails and entered once more among the live oaks where Spanish moss swayed in the sea wind. Our stay at the island was over until another year.

* * * * * * * * *

One needs to return to a good place. First explorations are exciting, but once one has learned where to go and how to get there, one has the chance of finding a great deal more; that is if one happens to be a naturalist.

Our second visit to Sapelo was in February of the following year. Jane and I had expected grey, cold days but found the winter so mild that red bud, jasmine, camelias and briars were all in bloom. This time we stayed in an apartment once used by the personnel of the estate. We liked it because it was close to the salt marsh with a tidal creek coming in to a boat landing.

* * * * * * * * *

I set out in the dim light before dawn for the loblolly grove beyond the pond with its coot and gallinule. A large bird sailed over my head as I entered the pines. What could it be? It alighted on an open pine limb. As its head swiveled 90-degrees to look at me, I saw that it was a Great Horned Owl.

A few mornings later dusk was thinning as I again skirted the pond. Mist hung low among the loblollies.

I could barely distinguish the white flags of deer bounding away. Then from the mistiness of the darkish pines came the repeated "who-hoo-hoo-hoo" with an extra "hoo" added beyond the usual call. I could see the outline of the Great Horned Owl, bending forward as it gave each hoot.

The owl was in the grove on other mornings. Once I heard an odd noise I could not place nor can I now describe, other than to say it was a wailing, shrill "uk" drawn out into an "u-u-k". The owl was apparently making the sound, for it moved whenever he did. But the bird seemed to be something of a ventriloquist: it was difficult to locate the sound precisely. I supposed that a nest must be nearby.

On that particular morning I had a fine view of the owl and could plainly see its white throat, white down the center of the breast and belly and the white feathers of its feet and talons. Five minutes after the Great Horned Owl became silent a Red-shouldered Hawk began screaming. A shift from nocturnal to diurnal predators had taken place.

The series of dead pines in the center of the grove that I had found the year before had been cut down. If left standing they might have furnished homes for Wood Duck, Bluebirds, Crested Flycatchers, Red-bellied and Pileated Woodpeckers and other hole-nesting birds. I have thought, at times, of writing an article entitled "O Woodsman, Spare that Dead Tree" so important are dead trees to wildlife.

But who am I to be taking up causes? As Sir Thomas Browne remarked centuries ago, we do not all have a genius for disputes. "A man may be in as just possession of truth as of a city," said he, "and yet be forced to surrender. 'Tis, therefore, far better to

enjoy her with peace than to hazard her on a battle."
Is it not best to enjoy what we have?

What was left in the grove was a dead top on a
living pine and it was in this that I found the male
Pileated roosting. Each morning after the owl had left
and the Red-bellied Woodpeckers had given their
first "kwirrs", the Pileated came out to be soon joined
by his mate who roosted at a distance. Then their day
began as did mine of watching.

It is difficult in most places to follow Pileated
Woodpeckers for long stretches of time. At Sapelo,
thanks to the open nature of the estate, I could follow
them for two or three hours before they took off on a
long flight. I then returned to our apartment by the
tidal creek to write up their feeding, courtship and
other habits; there is so much to learn and record
when one gets to studying the behavior of any particular bird.

* * * * * * * * *

The tide was down in the marsh when I set out for
an afternoon walk. Three male Boat-tailed Grackles
were displaying on the roof of the boat house, their
bills pointed upward. Another was walking along a
mud flat at the water's edge. A Snowy Egret stalked
prey in the shallows, the sun behind and its shadow
moving ahead. It held neck and head low, jabbing at
prey too small for me to see. One cormorant, farther
out, took flight with much pattering across the water.

I loved to visit the live oaks beyond the marsh when
the sun was high. One had glimpses of blue sky and
white clouds on looking up through branches. Shafts
of sunlight came down on the red bud and camelias.
The sun was behind me when I located the pair of

Pileated Woodpeckers. The female poked her bill
into a bed of resurrection ferns on an arching trunk
when the male appeared silently three feet away.

The pair, illuminated by a patch of sunlight, came
close, nearly touched bills, then separated. The
beauty of the birds and the closeness of their pair
bond were emphasized by the beauty of the background. I recalled descriptions of rain forests in the
tropics and came to think of the grove of live oaks as
being my "Green Mansions".

* * * * * * * * * *

There was much to look at high in the loblolly pines
where the Pileated had its roost hole, especially if one
reclined in a spot favorable to upward gaze. One afternoon a female Red-bellied Woodpecker rested
calm and composed on the upright part of a pine
limb. The male was resting not far away. These birds
appear to have life so arranged that they have more
leisure than most woodpeckers. This may be from
their generalized feeding habits and ability to store
food.

Beyond the pair a flock of Pine Siskins were feeding on the pollen, shed in profusion by the loblollies.
A sudden gust sent the pollen out in a yellow cloud.
Closer at hand a Bluebird was clinging to a pine trunk
as it scanned the ground, head to one side. A bird I
delighted in finding was the Yellow-throated Warbler, especially when it was probing into a streamer of
Spanish moss.

The bird I sought—a Brown-headed Nuthatch—
finally came into sight, its course marked by falling
flakes of bark as it investigated branches of the loblollies. Jane and I spent much time watching these
nuthatches in their usually unsuccessful attempts to
excavate nest holes.

An odd event had happened to this pair a few days before. I had discovered the nuthatch's nest hole high in a broken, semi-rotten pine limb at a time when the female Pileated was feeding nearby. When she flew to the nuthatch pine the wee birds became much excited. What a contrast in size! From the way the Pileated swung her head and knocked off chunks of dead wood, it was obvious that only a few blows—made in search of prey—would be enough to demolish the cavity made by the nuthatches.

The nuthatches swooped but the woodpecker seemed little concerned. In a sudden move the Pileated alighted above the nuthatches' nest cavity, raising her bill to strike. Each time she did so, one of the nuthatches swooped and the Pileated held her bill in an attempt to protect herself. The little birds persisted and the woodpecker never got a chance to strike the blow that might have demolished their nest. After a few minutes the Pileated flew to another pine.

Late in the afternoon I was again seated below and at a distance from the roost hole of the Pileated. Minutes passed. When would the male fly in from some part of his territory to roost for the night?

It was always a dramatic event when he arrived. His behavior was never quite the same on any two evenings. On this evening he alighted by his hole, put his head in, pulled it out, then backed down to drum a burst on the side. He seemed hesitant about entering for the night. He finally entered, but was soon looking out and giving a series of loud "cuks". Did he see something I did not see?

The sun had just left the tops of the tallest pines when I happened to notice the Great Horned Owl as it glided into the grove to perch on an open limb. It turned its head, glancing toward me. After a pause the owl took another glide in the direction of the live oaks, perhaps interested in grey squirrels living there.

The Pileated, head well out, followed the owl's every move. When the owl finally left the woodpecker disappeared into the darkness of his roosting place. Another shift had taken place. It was the time when the creatures of the night were beginning to replace those of the day. I thought of the lines from Macbeth: "Things of day begin to droop and drowse whilst night's black agents to their preys do rouse."

The trouble was, of course, that the Pileated was nearly all black and the owl, when I had seen it close and facing me, had much white in its plumage. Then again, I could not think of Great Horned Owls as being black agents. Our two Great Horneds in the library (see Chapter 15) had been house pets too long for me to consider them sinister. They had been so gentle with each other.

Shakespeare, nonetheless, gives a sense of the shift from day to night. I was grateful to the owl—seeing it as I did in the early morning and again at dusk—for a presentiment that there was much on the island that I, as a naturalist, was missing.

Some day, perhaps, I will return, change my sleeping habits, and learn how the other half of the world lives on this island paradise off Georgia.

IV. JUNE ON A MAINE ISLAND

"–To live in quiet on a plot of land surrounded by the sea, some island which they might learn to know thoroughly, that would not be too large to be explored easily and small enough to be loved dearly."–R. M. Lockley.

I believe it was Leonardo who implied that great things are done in small rooms or dwellings. Having done nothing great I cannot speak at first hand. But I have had great thoughts while living in a rough-board cabin with a stone fireplace off the Maine coast, especially after a day in the sea air.

Jane and I tossed our gear onto the rocks below the cabin one afternoon in June when the path leading to it was bright with hundreds of bunchberries in bloom. We had seen something of the island from the dory that brought us in. These were glimpses, between showers of salt spray, of the 80-acre island covered with hemlocks and beeches, with a fringe of spruce and balsam along the shore. The cabin at one end was the only habitation. But that is far from saying this island in Casco Bay was uninhabited.

A gentle rain had soaked the woods by the following morning. I have long had a love for building paths and this seemed like a time to cut one—a way of making myself at home regardless of weather. The path was projected to cross the island from the cabin

to the eastern shore. Part of the way I cut lower limbs
from spruce trees. Then I sawed up fallen balsams,
their black limbs festooned with clusters of *usnea*
moss. In other places I did no more than tramp a way
through beds of hay-scented ferns.

Making paths may represent an ancient instinct.
Konrad Lorenz tells of how a water shrew made paths
and assumed path-habits in a small aquarium. After a
few days on the island, Jane and I found ourselves
forming path habits of where we wanted to go. This
was especially true of the new trail, that I followed
each morning to watch the sun rise over the island-
studded bay.

One could never approach the opening at the end
of the trail too cautiously. Hearing a yodeling I could
not place, I stepped carefully over an old Indian clam
heap and parted the bayberry bushes. I saw one loon,
then another, coasting on a sea as smooth and reflect-
ing as a millpond. The early sun gleamed on their
white breasts as one raised its head to give a single,
wavering cry. Each loon left a line of ripples in the
water, the lines converging as they drifted together
and were joined by a third. The trio continued to
swim in and out among each other, turning heads as
they passed.

First one then another dipped its head under
water, as if the habit were contagious. The three
swam in still closer, seemingly curious, then gradually
separated and left. So much of the lives of these sea
birds is leisure! I seldom saw loons dive for fish and
supposed that in a short period they could catch all
they needed.

I turned my glass to the seaweed-covered ledges,
still showing above the incoming tide. Five seals were
swimming about, two of them mothers with half-

grown pups. When a mother's head broke the surface the head of her pup bobbed up beside her. The two heads nudged together, a way, no doubt, of demonstrating the bond between them.

A seal's head looks like that of a large dog when it first comes up. But when the animal floats, as it often does, with its head pointed straight up, the head comes to look more like an amorphous sea cucumber—an odd shape bobbing in swirls of tide. A seal might just sink in submerging, or again roll forward like a dolphin, with a sound of splashing coming over the bay. At times, when one floated straight out like a log, I was reminded of a beaver on its pond. The illusion was only momentary for the seals, unlike beaver, kept rolling about.

* * * * * * * * * *

I was exploring along the west shore when I came to a huge hemlock whose circle of branches had kept other trees from growing. Having a chance to glance

around, I looked upward into a large white pine, its branches made angular by the winds. This was why a pair of Ospreys had chosen it for their bulky nest. I had come quietly through the woods and one Osprey was so engaged in preening its feathers that it re-

mained unaware of my presence. I had time to unfold
my chair and watch at my ease.

Another minute passed before the Osprey began a
series of rapid peering motions as its head moved
jerkily from one side, then to the other, in a swing of
four to five inches. Its head remained upright the
whole time due to the flexibility of its longish neck.
For all this odd peering, the Osprey still failed to see
me. In minutes that followed it reached out with one
claw, scratched its head, preened again, then flew off
over the bay.

I continued walking to the colony of nesting Great
Blue Herons. This was the scene of the greatest activity on the island. I only skirted the colony on this
morning, listening to the sounds and disturbing the
birds as little as possible. There was always at least one
heron arriving or leaving, making, in either case, the
same guttural "k-wack, k'wack" sounds as it lumbered
over the treetops. The steady background din was a

pulsating "chirr, chirr, chirr, chirr" of what may have
been over a hundred half-grown young. They stood
or crouched on their bulky nests of sticks, surveying a
scene of devastation.

The excreta of the nesting herons was a defoliant
and tree-killer of the first order. Only one shrub survived, a red elder that throve in almost pure culture
below the blasted skeletons of the beeches, white
birch, spruces and other trees that had succumbed to
the birds.

The longer I sat the more varied became the noises
of the colony. It was like waiting at a zoo. There were
loud "grr-ok, grr-ok" sounds, for instance, reminding
one of lions and tigers getting warmed up (but with
the herons the final *dénouement* never came off). Just
as one expected a crescendo there might be a switch
to entirely different sounds,—long, drawn-out tubu-
lar ones: "qu-wh, wh-wk", hoarse and guttural, accompanied at times by sharper "scree-ee-awks".
Higher-pitched sounds in between, came I supposed,
from the young.

It was hard to believe that this cacaphony all came
from one species of bird. One might have expected to
see oddities drawn from all over the world, as in the
aviary of the Zoological Park in Washington. It was a
strange sensation to come upon such a metropolis
while rambling around a lonely Maine island on a
quiet morning in June.

The following morning I went again to the seal
look-out. "Unless you expect the unexpected," wrote
Heraclitus many years ago, "you will never find the
truth for it is hard to discover". I would modify this to
say, "never find all that goes on in nature".

As I approached the shore with this caution in
mind, I tried to gear myself for something unex-

pected. It came in the form of a mournful "wow".
What could it be?

Being from inland, I was learning how seals communicate when undisturbed. Then came some low
"quocks", a sound I recognized as that of eider ducks.
There was a cluster of a dozen females not far from
shore, followed by a trail of perhaps 40 ducklings—
one large communal family. Once I settled down, the
ducklings began diving around the submerged sea-
weed of the seal's ledge, their webbed feet appearing
for an instant as their bodies plunged bottoms up.
Seals came close, but the ducklings remained undisturbed until a large head bobbed up among them.
Then they scooted to their communal mothers and
aunts.

Jane and I met on the cabin porch at seven o'clock.
As is our custom, she had walked one way and I
another, so that each of us had news to communicate.
I learned the whereabouts of some flowers and the
nest of a White-throated Sparrow I had missed. Both
of us had discovered the nest of a Black Duck with
eight eggs.

The bay below the porch remained placid as a
millpond in the incoming tide. A toy-like "bup", a
pleasant sound, kept coming to us over the water.
Then we saw a flotilla of seven loons. As they came
nearer their wakes criss-crossed into a diamond lattice
of ripples. The "bup" note of these birds—birds that
like to gather sociably, then drift away—was to become a familiar feature of our island life . . . a life
short in days but long in peaceful experience.

* * * * * * * * * *

I arose in the morning thinking of Thoreau's remark that "That day only dawns to which we are

awake". Thoreau might never have approved of my way of awakening at the island. I liked to get up in the dark, a few hours before dawn, build a fire of beech wood, then enjoy several cups of coffee—"that muddy stimulant" as Thoreau might have called it— before writing my journal of our previous day's adventures. This gave me a feeling of beginning the day with a margin of leisure.

Coffee in hand and looking in the fire, I saw the string of eider ducklings following each other as the sun rose among the islands; the baby seal bobbing up close to nudge its mother;—the sociable loons circling lazily in their water minuet. Each creature had been communicating the bonds that brought them close. Perhaps not great thoughts, I reminded myself—but pleasant ones.

Still in imagination I saw a Black-backed Gull sail in a long glide against a background of pointed firs along the shore, to land on a little rock by itself. After a wriggle to adjust its wings, it rested in the first rays of the early sun. What peace, what contentedness! To be able just to rest minute after minute in perfect calm, a calm matching that of the incoming tide and the warmth of the sun flooding one side of the island.

What a feeling to share on quiet days! Sensing the larger bond one can have with nature on a Maine island, I reached for my journal while the inspiration—and the coffee—lasted.

V. THE BEACH

"Great ocean beach runs north and south unbroken, mile lengthening into mile. Solitary and elemental, unsullied and remote, visited and possessed by the outer sea." Henry Beston.

"All memorable events, I should say, transpire in morning time, and in a morning atmosphere." H. D. Thoreau.

I have long thought of Henry Beston and his small house on the dunes of Cape Cod. I read the book when it first came out and have re-read it many times since.

How well would I have made out, had someone lent me the house when I was of college age? As Beston observed, "It is not easy to live alone, for a man is a gregarious creature; especially in his youth, powerful instincts offer battle to such a way of life, and in utter solitude odd things may happen to the mind." In years of college and after, I did not have the peace of mind, the freedom from trying to find a place in the world one needs in order to live in the presence of nature.

How different, and for the better, things look at age 65! We talk too much of youth and age. It is not so much a matter of how many or how few years, but of inner peace. One's mind has to be at rest. Only then can one equilibrate with the beauty of the universe.

Some express these things when they are young. Wordsworth did; so did Richard Jeffries, Thoreau and Henry Beston. But in a crowded world there is always the conflict between one's love of nature and the demands of society. I never felt free for long.

Our senses are keener when we are young but one needs—or, at least, I needed—accumulated wisdom to stand aside. Some develop later than others; some never find themselves. At threescore-years-and-five I find that I now experience the joy that comes from natural things more continuously, and with more freedom, than I did when young. For a naturalist, the last of life—to paraphrase Robert Browning—can be the part for which "the first was made."

* * * * * * * * * *

There is an ever-present friendliness in the sea beach at Sapelo that Jane and I have shared on many visits. When there, we often walked our separate ways. This is because—as any true walker such as Hazlett, Robert Louis Stevenson or Thoreau will attest—the mind and eye need absolute freedom if one is to get the most from a walk. No two individuals, even man and wife, are likely to enjoy nature in the same way from moment to moment. One will prefer to pause here, another there, or to stroll at a faster or slower pace.

By doing so we have the added pleasure of exchanging notes on what we have seen when our paths cross. Jane, watching by the nest of the Pileated Woodpecker, made sketches of two fledging Great Horned Owls, a high point of her morning. While walking along the beach during the same time, I enjoyed the play of dolphins close in shore. With shared experiences we learned and anticipated more. The island became more alive.

* * * * * * * * *

One of the sights along the beach were Brown Pelicans whose activities varied with wind and tide. The waves on March 19, with an onshore wind, were as high as any I had seen. I did not need to beat along the beach to see birds. They were all on the wing and I saw them well enough from where I stood—small, fast-flying Dunlin, single Herring Gulls, three scaup ducks and a Snowy Egret. Best of all were the pelicans. They came by so low over the waves and so close as to be hidden part of the time by the rising wall of breakers.

A first group was followed after an interval by six more, riding by with an alternation of slow flaps and long easy glides on huge, outstretched wings. They rode the currents as comfortably as a baby in a pram. Their ungainly heads had a benign, placid look, contrasting with the turbulence around them—a grand spectacle against the background of such a sea.

March 20, with a stiff offshore wind blowing spray and breakers seaward, was the reverse of the day before. I had not sat long before I again saw pelicans approaching. They came by in well-separated groups of three close in among the breakers—smooth, effortless glides with wings turned down at the tips, one pelican close behind the other. They looked to be having a wonderful time, as skiiers might on a downhill slope. Theirs is a skill inborn. Were they gliding in play or were they going somewhere?

I closed my eyes to better feel the wind on my face and hear the roar and tumult of the waves, letting my imagination carry me as though I too were being borne aloft. Imagine living day after day as our ancestors did for millions of years, like the pelicans and other creatures, exposed and one with the elements, whatever the day might bring by way of wind, wave, sun or rain.

On the following day the sea was flat with only a single line of breakers—not nearly as stirring as when whipped by the wind. The tide was partly down and the beach a glare of sunlight. The pelicans were close to shore, this time sailing and flapping about six feet over the water, pausing to dive when seeing a fish. With feet out and wings half spread, they hit the water so gently that no more than heads, necks and bills went under. I could see their distended pouches as they emerged. What jolly looking birds! Pelicans are clumsy and ungainly to look at, but masters in their way of life.

A strong wind was blowing directly up the beach on March 22. The ocean was at half tide. Sanderling pattered along the freshly wet sand while, at the other extreme, pelicans were diving off shore. The pelicans were taking high plunges, disappearing under the waves as their bodies shot up columns of spray. Having now watched them over four succeeding days, I hoped that I would be able to follow their activities on still further mornings. But they moved elsewhere and we saw no more of them.

It is the variety of the sea that appeals to inlanders. At no time did Jane and I feel this more than our visits to the beach at dawn. Our senses were then freshest and we felt the sea the most, as the following journal entries will hopefully attest.

23 March

Banks of fog make the sun a round disc sending a path of golden reflections across the waves to the beach. The tide is still high but going out. A few gulls are overhead. Several Dunlin wing fast over the water edge. How quietly the day begins! An Indian might have once stood on the beach, hands outward to the sun. One needs to go back to earlier days to be a part of this beautiful world of mists, low-lapping breakers, sea birds and endless stretches of wave-washed sand.

2 April

How I love the first roar of surf as I walk through the strip of dunes to the beach! This morning the wind comes direct from the sea; moist, invigorating. Grey clouds continue but always the length, breadth and stir of the beach and ocean make a wonderful horizon.

A pair of Willets stand in a shallow dip of water left by the receding tide, preening small feathers of breasts and bellies as well as the longer ones of their wings. It is peculiar the way they continually dip bills into the salt water, then run them through their plumage. Are they preening with salt water and sand? If so, why not bathe directly?

This grey morning a single Black Skimmer sails back and forth over the inner line of surf (almost a misnomer when breakers are only four inches high). The skimmer flies in easy flight, its long black wings keeping it at just the right height. Its hanging lower mandible furrows the water in front of the curl of a breaker.

Why does a bird moving at such speed not wreck itself? Supposing the dangling mandible caught on some shell or piece of sea wrack? But the long, graceful wings compensate for the myriad variations of wind and wave as the bill holds its steady course. Skimmers have little in the way of a tail to guide them: their skill is in their wings. To see a line of five or six of these striking black and white birds, beating along one behind the other and so close to the waters edge is one of the grand sights of the beach.

3 April

This is a dawn of extraordinary sky effects but the beach at low tide appears bleak and lifeless as Jane and I first cross the dunes. A strong wind is blowing storm clouds from the southwest. Fine sheets of sand travel by our feet to disappear as they hit wet places farther on. A poor morning, I think, too grey and windy.

Then suddenly the sky changes to the seaward. Patches of white clouds, tinted underneath with saffron from the rising sun, appear well above the low ones of the overcast. Among them I have a glimpse of blue sky and a half moon.

To the landward, at the same time, the line of dunes and beach grass look especially fine against a background of black clouds—the threat of an oncoming deluge. Two kinds of sky today: one of the approaching cloudburst, the other, to the seaward (at least, in brief glimpses) of a fine morning with blue sky and sunshine.

Jane is now a receding figure walking well up the beach, heading toward the nest of our Pileated Woodpecker via the sea route. She meets the center of the deluge when it breaks.

As I enjoy the spectacle around me, I see the dark fin of a bottlenose dolphin roll into view then disappear remarkably close to the beach. How can these great creatures maneuver in such shallow water?

The dolphins pass and I believe the show has ended. Then I see an extraordinary sight as three dolphins begin to mill about in one place. Three times one or another of them leaps clear of the water, falling back each time with a splash. I see the white belly of one several times and, once, a fluke waving in the air. What is the excitement?

My thoughts (strengthened later in talking with others) are that I have been watching courtship, known to take place in shallow water.

The sky effects, the cloudburst, the dolphins; what variety the beach and sea offer!

4 April

There is a new moon on this, our coldest morning. The sky is clear, with a cold west wind. I have on my warmest clothing,—long johns, a scarf, wind-breaker, and gloves. The beach is almost barren of bird life at low tide. Its cold, severe look is more like outer Cape Cod in winter than a sea island off Georgia.

My watch reads ten past seven as the sun pops out of the sea, round and clear. This morning, I think,

will be a bleak one for birds. Little is likely to happen.
Then, as I look seaward, a dark mass shimmers low
over the waves. A mirage? I look more closely and
distinguish a string of cormorants dark against the
sun, migrating northward. A few others come by
closer too. They have strong wing beats and are
steady flyers for birds so adapted to swimming and
diving.

Then I become aware of hundreds more cormorants approaching from the south—a veritable boiling
up of birds; an irregular, stringy black mass moving
northward. They pass the orange orb of the sun, still
not above the waves, in a long single line extending
way up the beach. There is the beating of hundreds
of wings, the pulse of a great migration.

* * * * * * * * * *

Is the world overcrowded? Are there no places for
solitude—places where one can be alone for a time
with incoming waves, sea birds, and vast stretches of
sand?

Much, I think, depends on the time one arises. Jane
and I were always up early and at the beach by dawn,
never seeing anyone there in what, for us, was the
grandest hour of the day. No plane passing overhead
disturbed the endless sounds of nature. The beach
was ours.

"Dwelling thus upon the dunes," wrote Beston, "I
lived in the midst of an abundance of natural life
which manifested itself every hour of the day, and
from being thus surrounded, thus enclosed within a
great whirl of energy. There were times, on the
threshold of spring, when the force seemed as real as
heat from the sun. A skeptic may smile and ask me to
come to his laboratory and demonstrate; he may talk

as he will of the secret workings of my own isolated and uninfluenced flesh and blood, but I think that those who have lived in nature, and tried to open their doors rather than close them on her energies, will understand well enough what I mean. Life is as much a force in the universe as electricity or gravitational pull, and presence of life sustains life."

VI. FOX CUBS BY THE BEARCAMP POND

"I could turn and live with animals."–Walt Whitman.

I was paddling my canoe along the shore of Bear-Bearcamp Pond near the White Mountains of New Hampshire, admiring the shadbushes in bloom and watching for birds of the May migration. A grey Marsh Hawk, in gull-like flight, followed the shore line around a point of pines.

I paddled over to the land there, wanting to walk along wood road that led to a lumber clearing with its sawdust pile. As I approached, a small animal trotted down the road toward me, his wobbly gait giving him an odd appearance.

I saw with field glasses that this small fox was young enough to have soft, wooly, red-brown fur. His legs and tail were black but the tip of his tail had an inch of white. I stood still to watch: if there was one fox, there must be more. Sure enough, another youngster soon came wobbling up to nose the first.

Then I found a third curled asleep on the grass! I edged closer, a few inches at a time. One cub took alarm and went behind a pine stump to a pile of slash and peered at me from there. The brush pile, with its many approaches, was apparently the foxes' den. They crawled in and out of it during my subsequent

visits. I supposed that there might be a hole, or burrow, concealed in the center of it. If there was such, it
must have been damp for the pile itself was only
slightly above a pool full of croaking frogs.

I discovered a fourth cub near a pine stump, curled
head to tail and sound asleep on the sawdust pile. He
awoke as I approached. Instead of running away he
backed down the pile, seemingly incredulous of his
first view of man. He led my glance to the last of the
five, still asleep on the pine log staging.

Having no desire to frighten the cubs, as I wished
to return later for photographs, I walked back to the
shore. It was a bit careless, I thought, for the family of
foxes to stay out in the open. They might fall prey to
hawks and other predators.

There were no foxes in sight on my return the
following morning, so I contented myself with watching a noisy Olive-sided Flycatcher as it flew from one
dead treetop to another. The clearing resounded
with songs of White-throated Sparrows. Among these
I spotted one of their northern relatives, a beautiful
White-crowned.

The next afternoon an Osprey flew from a dead tree near the pine stump. With the help of my binoculars I located three of the foxes rambling near their brush pile. Although I spent several hours watching and photographing, the other two never appeared. My fears about the hawks may well have been justified. A small fox would make as good prey as a rabbit.

Taking off my shoes, I cautiously stalked a sleeping cub with my camera. When I crunched a leaf he looked up sleepily as though to say "go away", and then resettled himself to continue his snooze. The foxes slept with both eyes closed. When I finally got within ten feet the cub sat up for a few minutes of vigorous scratching with a hind leg, interspersed with some deep yawns. I do not know whether it was my intrusion or small parasites next to his skin that caused him to crawl back under the pile of brush.

Soon after I found three of the foxes curled up in a mass looking, in my finder, as if they had been up late the night before.

* * * * * * * * *

It was with a different purpose that I visited the clearing several days later. We had decided to get rid of porcupines that had been gathering under our summer house. Porcupines in the woods are interesting enough, but sharing a place with them is difficult. Their constant gnawing at the underpinnings of the house not only threatened the structure, but kept us awake at night. Nor was this all. Equally distressing was the partial destruction of a huge tamarack tree that was a landmark of our clearing.

The last straws were when a porcupine gnawed the telephone line in two as well as completing a hole in the floor large enough for our ice box to fall through.

Traps seemed the quickest solution, but oh how I was to regret having used one! All I caught was a beautiful snowshoe hare which still had a patch of winter white in its fur. What an unfortunate event! While wondering what to do with the carcass, I thought of the foxes. What a good dinner it would make for them.

I went again to the sawdust pile. The White-throated Sparrows were singing, the hobblebush was still in bloom—but not a fox was in sight. I decided to explore the neighboring marsh for a bit before returning. Meanwhile I set the rabbit by the big pine stump. What a picture it would make with all the foxes tugging at it! Of course the mother fox, scenting human hands, might keep her cubs away. But, so far mother fox seemed to be following a policy of *laissez-faire*.

Life in the marsh was most interesting. Solitary Sandpipers ran along the water's edge and an Osprey screamed as it circled overhead. I found five huge snapping turtles in as many minutes, all lumbering about in shallow water.

Thus it was an hour before I returned to the big pine stump. The rabbit was gone and I could not see any foxes. Then I became aware of all sorts of noises under the brush heap—tugging, scuffling and the distinct crunching of bones. Now and then a little snout would poke out through the branches, only to quickly return to the feast. Here, I thought, was my chance for photos. Stuffed with the dinner I had provided, the foxes would feel like nothing more than a comfortable snooze in the sun!

No such luck! When they emerged the foxes were full of urgings to go places and do things. One fell off a grass tuft into the frog pool. He did not seem to like the water. Another, more adventurous, ran up the trunk of a slanting tree until he was quite high off the ground—I stood at the base to cut off his retreat.

What would he do? The cub came down to a lower level and laid his nose close to the bark, looking straight up at me with his yellow eyes. It was no longer the look of an innocent wooly cub. Those slanting eyes had become sly and cunning as he planned his escape. This he achieved quite simply by dropping into the water and disappearing among the roots of an upturned stump.

The last I saw of the family was another young fox trotting off into the woods. The cubs had matured a lot in the four days I had known them, their early *insouciance* having given way to the alertness all wild animals must develop to survive. How lucky I was to have found them at just the right time! Had I come through the lumber clearing a week later, I might never have suspected how much was going on there.

VII. WATCHING MAMMALS

"I still go on the principle that if you are watching the higher animals, watch them as if there were people."
F. Fraser Darling

One autumn day I set out against the wind to look for mammals along the edge of Seneca Swamp. The rattling of dry cornstalks covered the noise of my footsteps as the steady breezes carried away my scent. Perhaps that's why the grey fox, hunting and running about in search of prey, paid little or no attention to me. He was a beautiful creature at close range; the grey, white-tipped fur of his back, a warm, reddish patch along the throat with white underneath, and a black-tipped tail . . . but it was such a difficult place to stalk that I soon lost him.

Many times I have crept quite close to foxes. Once, keeping behind boulders and bushes, I sneaked up to within 20 feet of a red fox in a hayfield and watched as he caught beetles and crickets by jumping on them—almost playfully—with his front feet.

Wild animals observed closely and left undisturbed are beautiful, alert, friendly and playful. Those who know mammals only from seeing them when cornered or frightened can little appreciate how attractive they are.

* * * * * * * * *

A special fondness for raccoons goes back to a June afternoon in New Hampshire some years ago. I was listening to the songs of White-throated Sparrows and Chestnut-sided Warblers in our clearing when a sudden strange cry led me to reach for my field glasses and head for the woods.

I followed the noise down a rain-water brook to a huge old sugar maple with only a few live branches remaining on its rotting trunk. A baby racoon clung to one of these, too small to climb either up or down. Luckily for him his mother came to the rescue, hitching up the broad trunk like a porcupine. Seizing the baby in her teeth she carried him up to a cavernous hole into which they both disappeared. I thought this was the last I would see of them for, like many mammals, raccoons come out mostly at night.

But a few nights later something raided a collection of small animals that Jane, I, and the children had made in the barn. In the morning all we found were empty containers where earlier wood mice, shrews, frogs and turtles, the results of our forays in swamps and woods, had lived.

That night I tied some fish to a piece of fence-wire on our cabin porch so that any animal jolting it would waken us. When the wire rattled some hours later, Jane and I turned on flashlights to watch a raccoon finishing the fish. It is amazing that while slight noises may put wild mammals to flight, a light turned directly on them may frighten them little if at all.

Within a week our raccoon was paying regular visits to the porch to the delight of our entire family. Edging closer each night, the animal and I gained bravado. I was soon feeding the raccoon scraps with a fork, not using my fingers for fear it might consider them as fresh meat.

It soon became apparent that our visitor was a nursing mother. One night, hearing low, purring noises, I turned on the flashlight and found the raccoon guarding four tiny youngsters. When I followed her around the corner of the house, the young crowded close as she snarled at me. I wanted to pick one up but I had no wish to break the confidence of the mother who had brought her family to us.

All through the remaining nights of our vacation the raccoon, her ravenous appetite fostered by nursing young, became increasingly bold. If the door were open she would steal to the dining table, stand up with her front paws on its edge, then hoist herself up.

She enjoyed bread and ate butter separately. Jane, watching with flashlight in hand, noticed that the raccoon delicately unwrapped a new loaf rather than tear the paper.

When we shut the door, hoping to bar further visits and to get some sleep, the raccoon went around and came in by a back window. We then shut everything possible, thinking she would go elsewhere. Instead she climbed to the roof and walked back and forth, making us wonder whether she might come down the chimney.

If I lived in the country year-round I would maintain a nocturnal feeding station to attract wild animals. It is one of the easiest ways to watch them provided one is ready to sacrifice a little sleep.

* * * * * * * * * *

Our old apple trees attracted Ruffed Grouse, deer and sometimes, bear. One fall I spotted long scratches and freshly broken branches on a tree close to our cabin where a bear had been after apples.

Deer followed a nightly route close to the apple tree.

In winter, tracks in the snow made this obvious, while in summer their barking awakened us as they passed in the night.

Like many wild mammals, deer rely on their noses and ears to warn them of danger, their eyesight being relatively poor. I have often stalked close to deer when the wind was right by moving only when their heads were down. One October morning a doe did the reverse as far as I was concerned. Curious to know what I was as I stood still and gave her no clue, she slowly came to within 30 feet. Then, moving

along in a semi-circle, she finally picked up my scent
and bounded away.

* * * * * * * * * *

Of all woodland creatures, none are more unfairly
condemned than skunks. They are actually mild, inoffensive animals, ejecting their scent only when
frightened.

One is apt to meet them on evening walks through
the fields. By moving cautiously I have walked to
within eight feet while watching one hunt for its supper in the grass. Standing still, I once had one run up
to within a foot of me without being startled.

Skunks investigate every inch of the terrain with a
rapid, continual sniffing. Those I have watched have
caught nothing but insects, but they do, of course, eat
other things as well. When beginning to get alarmed,
they stamp by bringing both front feet down on the
ground in a signal that should be sufficient warning. I
have watched chamois in the Alps do the same thing
when excited.

One way to learn something about a mammal's
character is to keep one around the house as a pet.
Jimmy, our hand-raised skunk, lived with us for al-

most a year. He devoured mice and Domestic Sparrows as well as dog food, but nothing stimulated him as much as an insect. He would quiver with excitement if I put a beetle nearby, showing surprising agility in pinning it down with his forepaws. If given a wooly bear caterpillar with hairs like a bristle brush, Jimmy would roll it back and forth for some minutes in his forepaws until the hairs had fallen loose, before devouring the body.

He ate enormously in fall months and became as fat as a butter ball.

Jimmy enjoyed having his fur stroked while he dozed in one's lap. Like cats, skunks are clean animals and learn to use a sandbox. Jimmy never scratched the upholstery. As a pet, Jimmy was nonetheless, peculiar in some ways. Although tamed, he reverted to wild state when out-of-doors, apparently feeling secure only when running around the house where he knew every corner.

* * * * * * * * * *

To see an animal dash off in flight may be interesting enough, and this glimpse is all that people are likely to get while in talkative groups or walking with dogs. Considerable satisfiaction may come from observing wildlife undisturbed.

One evening I went to Great Hill Pond in New Hampshire to see what luck I might have with beaver. The moment I reached the shore a beaver swam past with its head bobbing periodically like a swimmer doing the breast stroke. I followed along the edge of the pond as it swam around a point of land. Hearing a gnawing sound I removed my shoes and socks and— keeping away from sticks to minimize noises—I gradually worked to within 20 feet of a large beaver feeding on leaves and twigs of hobble-bushes (*Viburnum alnifolium*) then in bloom.

As I could not follow in the bushes I stood near an aspen felled by beaver and lying out over the water. The beaver ahead of me returned to the shore and swam to the aspen. Then she spanked the water with her tail and dove, only to come right up again.

I expected her to leave in alarm. Instead she bounced up on the water with both forelegs out, trying to grasp the crown of the aspen. I could see the beaver was a nursing mother and probably very hungry. After a number of trials she finally caught a branch and—to my surprise—brought it in her teeth to a muddy landing at my feet.

Coming out of the water she sat upright, propped by her broad tail and webbed hind feet as she rolled the branch in her forepaws to eat the bark. Her incisor teeth moved so rapidly that she reminded me of the noises logs make when fed to a saw mill. There were pauses while she chewed with her back teeth, almost smacking her lips as though the bark was delicious. I hoped, looking down, that she would not bring her long incisors any closer to my bare feet. But she paid no more attention to me then if I had been an old stump.

Well-covered with insect repellant, I was able to stand motionless for some time. When the stick was finally gnawed white and clean the beaver swam straight across the pond in the direction of her lodge.

* * * * * * * * * *

Some of my best views of mammals have been while bird watching. Once as I floated in a kayak along the edge of a New Hampshire pond trying to locate a

Kingbird's nest, I heard a splash and saw what I believed was a muskrat climbing onto the muddy shore.
Making hardly a ripple with my paddle, I drifted
until close enough to hear the animal crunching
something in its jaws. The creature was too large for a
muskrat, and did not have the shape of a beaver.

As it slipped into the water and swam alongside the
kayak, I saw it was an otter. It dove farther along, its
furry tail waving in the air as it went down.

A few days later I had an even more exciting experience. Jane and I were taking an evening walk
along a dirt road when I stopped to seek out a warbler
in a hemlock tree.

Jane suddenly whispered "bear . . . !"

We held our breaths as a black bear ambled along a
lumber track directly toward us. Two little cubs tumbled along behind, standing up on their hind legs to
examine sticks and flowers. When 14 steps away the
mother climbed on a log to sniff in our direction. She
seemed no larger than a big Newfoundland dog.

Catching our scent she ran off among the balsam
firs, the two cubs leaping over the log after her. The

cubs, less than a foot high and rather long-legged, seemed small. Neither Jane nor I thought for a moment that the mother bear was dangerous. We believed her one desire was to hustle her cubs away as fast as possible.

I learned from such experiences that one does not have to go into remote mountain wildernesses to see wildlife. There may be more to see close to home, if one goes out at the right time of day, makes no noise and is in no hurry. Under such circumstances one may have the good fortune to be accepted by wildlife as a part of the landscape. It is only then that wild creatures are seen at their best.

* * * * * * * * * *

Climbing Mt. Wonalancet in the White Mountains one May morning I hoped to find a Bay-breasted Warbler, expecting no unusual encounter with wild animals. On the summit ridge I located only Blackpoll and Magnolia Warblers.

In the stillness of the wind-stunted balsams I listened for the notes of other birds. Then I heard a weird, unplaceable noise. Curious, I followed it as rapidly as dead limbs and fallen trunks would allow. I thought the rather piercing notes might come from a nest of young hawks.

Within closer range the mixture of wails and grunts sounded more mammalian, like young bobcats tussling outside a den.

The slope here was steep with a jumble of moss-covered boulders. Sliding down carefully, I peered over a ledge. Below was a large, whittish porcupine—white due to a preponderance of long white quills—squatting on its hind legs and swaying slightly. Perhaps it was a mother nursing a young one and crooning to it in an odd sort of way. But as the porcupine turned, I saw that it had a few quills sticking out of its nose—wrong-end-to—and was rubbing at them ineffectively with its forepaws.

A few feet above the whitish animal perched a moderate-sized, blacker porcupine. This porky, mouth open and head forward, was making the noises, a series of lugubrious wails, squeals and grunts.

Apparently the two porcupines were fighting, for Whitie now closed for another round. The animals boxed with their forepaws as each tried to bite the other. Both quickly tired of the business, Whitie waddling off over the ledge. Blackie seemed too miserable to move.

The piteous calls persisted as I slid down to within five feet.

Blackie had a mouth so full of quills that he could not close it.

I took photographs from several angles. Instead of presenting a back of bristling quills, and the threat of a swish from his powerful tail as porcupines normally behave towards an intruder, Blackie simply faced me each time I moved. Then the obvious occurred to me. He wanted help. From his point of view I had turned up at just the right time.

I had neither forceps nor pliers and was more than a little wary of reaching between those powerful incisors with my fingers. So breaking off two small spruce sticks, I sidled up to my patient. I could not very well hold him as though he were a dog but, with a quick pull, I pulled a quill from his lower lip. Blackie never moved. Then in rapid succession I pulled the remaining quills from his palate.

Blackie made motions with his tongue and cheek as though to rinse his mouth. I thought he looked happier but, to be honest, he remained as expressionless as a log of wood.

Sitting beside the porcupine, I gave him a final inspection. All quills in sight now pointed outward, in proper fashion. It was the hairs in between that caught my attention. Each had one or more lice crawling on it, so that all seemed to move. Here was a chance for further treatment.

I reached for my small bottle of 6-12 insect repellent. But Blackie, now quite restored, began to scramble up the ledge. He paused a moment, gave me another dull look, then squeezed himself between two moss-covered granite boulders and disappeared.

The forest stillness was now broken only by the occasional call of a migrating Black-poll Warbler. Pleased that a porcupine had trusted me when in need I picked my way back to the trail.

* * * * * * * * * *

My knowledge of fishers was restricted to books until, late one fall, I saw one high on the slopes of Mount Moosilauke. It was running up a log in woods of spruce and fir close to the trail—a fine animal in brown fur with the body size of a cat.

It is often called a cat by the natives, but is not one. Nor is it a fisher in any literal sense. The native term "fisher cat", therefore, is a double misnomer. Fishers belong to the weasel family along with skunks and badgers and unlike their cousins, the mink and the otter, they do not catch fish.

A year passed before I found fresh tracks after a snowfall in December. The tracks seems to be those of a large male that had bounded in and out among balsams where snowshoe hares had runways. The fisher had also visited farther up on the land where porcupines denned among rocks. With later snowfalls the tracks disappeared only to appear again in late January, crossing the trail by the Pout Pond Brook no less than six times within a quarter-mile.

I had nearly forgotten about fishers when, in late winter, I walked to what Jane and I called the Big Woods. A snowfall of several inches had begun in the early morning and ended by 10:00 A.M., obliterating older tracks. I was therefore surprised to come upon an abundance of fisher tracks all in one place.

These were of two sizes. I supposed that the larger, nearly four inches in length, were those of a male and the smaller, half the size, those of a female. The animals had run side by side in an irregular course, opening up every three or four yards into areas containing hundreds of tracks. The snow was well trampled. Small bits of fur suggested that mating had been going on for it is a habit among members of the weasel family for males to seize females by the back of the neck (a love embrace to her). There were six of these trampled areas extending 25 yards from the base of a hollow basswood.

The fishers appeared to have scrambled up and down the base of the tree, leaving pieces of bark scattered on the snow. Looking up I noted a freshly-gnawed hole 15 feet above the ground. The hole was obviously an old one, part of a fissure running up and down the trunk. The fresh gnawings were superficial. Being only four inches wide by six deep the opening did not appear large enough for the male to enter. I wondered whether the female might not have selected it for this reason. It would keep her mate from entering and interfering with the young.

I continued to visit the basswood as time went by without finding any indication that it was being used for a den. But the spring snow was granular and unfavorable for tracking.

Jane was walking in the Big Woods at eight o'clock on the morning of April 7, just 17 days after the mating, when she heard what she thought was a porcupine scrambling up a tree. On coming closer, she found the noises were coming from inside the basswood—a medley of pipings and squeakings that reminded her of suckling ferrets, of which we had raised several litters.

As Jane looked up the mother fisher put her head out, showing a perfect profile. The nesting cavity was not dark within, for a crack just below the entrance admitted light. Jane estimated that the family of fishers were below this, occupying a cavity about three-and-a-half feet deep.

Female fishers have a gestation time of nearly a year so we wondered, in reconstructing events,

whether the fisher had not given birth in late March
and then mated.

We never found further indication of activity in the
basswood on subsequent visits. But considering how
secretive wild animals can be—especially when having
young—we have always regarded the fisher den as a
high point of walks in winter woods.

VIII. SMALL MAMMALS FROM EARTHY RUNWAYS

"Gnome-hunting has been my pastime."–Frank Bolles.

If one is a naturalist who wears old clothes and is ready to crawl on all fours to peer into holes in stumps, he will have an idea of the numbers of small mammals in woods and fields.

In any piece of natural woodland one has only to scoop away the carpet of dead leaves or to turn over a rotting log to find a good tunnel. They are everywhere. We may rarely see the gnomes which use them for they are most active at night. Yet one interested in mammalogy has ways of learning who they are.

When younger I used to set out with a small bag filled with single snap-over mouse traps, some strips of cloth, and a jar of bait. . . peanut butter, bacon and oatmeal made a good mixture.

Experience helped in knowing where to set the traps. A stone wall is particularly good as all manner of small mammals may run along beneath it, but one may have to dig at several spots before a well-worn runway comes to light. After setting several traps along a wall I might place one under a log or by an upturned stump. If a brooklet was nearby some over-hanging mossy bank or boulder made a suitable site. Strips of cloth tied to bushes aided in relocating the traps. A countryman seeing my traps drawled, "well, if he likes to catch mice, I guess he'll never want for sport!"

Visiting sets on the following day was exciting. Sometimes I caught little, but one must be prepared for that. At other times I found that under the stone wall I had captured a tiny grey mammal with a long tail, pointed snout and almost no eyes, a shorttail shrew and under a log a redback mouse.

Where the brooklet splashed down between mossy boulders and luxuriant ferns I caught a special prize, a creature with an exceedingly long tail tufted at the end, long legs like a kangaroo, light underparts and a dark brown back—a woodland jumping mouse.

I used to make museum skins out of such specimens, an art that takes experience. The specimens were helpful because many mice and shrews cannot be identified in life. I came to feel, nonetheless, that living creatures are more interesting than dead ones. Catching small mammals alive also requires more skill. One method is to use midget box traps; another to catch the creatures by hand when opportunity offers.

* * * * * * * * * *

One day in late April I opened the door of our New Hampshire ice house. In a corner of the sill was a nest of shredded sacking from which tumbled four blind, furry redback mice.

The mother put them back in the nest, showing little fear. I then put both hands over the nest and placed the whole family in an aquarium filled with four inches of fresh-smelling pine needles. A piece of wood and a weatherbeaten sheep's skull provided additional hideouts.

Mother mouse quickly built a series of tunnels, some of them running next to the glass so that I had a cross section of the forest floor for observation. Once the tunnels were done, the mother tore down the old nest and built a new, bulkier one in a corner.

I was soon feeding the mother peanut butter, oatmeal, carrot and meat scraps from my fingers. Sometimes she sat up on her hind legs to eat like a squirrel. When satisfied, she would hide the left-overs in the nest. The young mice were more timorous than their mother and squeaked like teddy bears when handled. But they were playful and investigative like all young animals and were cute when asleep with paws folded over each other. The mother meanwhile slept alone under the sheep's skull. She had learned that there was little rest for her in a nest full of young.

Two weeks later, when the young were grown, I returned the family, and their nest, to the ice house. Three days later I looked in to see how the mice were doing. A few were still there, but they showed little recognition of their former captor.

* * * * * * * * * *

Meadow mice are physically like redbacks but are grey-brown and larger.

Early one June when the water of Great Hill Pond lay quiet and dark without a ripple, I paddled my kayak with a minimum of noise so that I might listen to birds ashore. I heard the "rig-a-jig" of a Yellow-throat, the distant "cuk-cuk" of a Pileated Wood-pecker and the "wa-an" of a sapsucker.

Twenty feet ahead I noticed something swimming. It saw me and dove. On approaching I found a meadow mouse swimming six inches under the water, perhaps 70 feet from shore and apparently heading for an island. I put a paddle under and lifted it up to find that it had an air bubble over each eye. He scrambled to one end of the kayak and that was the last I saw of him. He apparently jumped overboard as I paddled along. I hoped that he would not fall prey to a pickerel or a snapping turtle before reaching the shore.

* * * * * * * * * *

Of all wild mice, the white-footed deer mouse is one of the prettiest and easiest to see. Although they lived in our yard in Bethesda, Maryland, we saw them to best advantage in our cabin in New Hampshire. One heard them stirring about as soon as the lights

were out. Then turning on a flashlight, we could see the white-foot with long whiskers, large deer-like eyes, soft brown back and snowy white underparts, sitting unafraid on a pantry shelf. Out-of-doors white-foots go jump, jump, jump over the dead leaves, so loud in the stillness as to suggest a much larger animal.

If one keeps these mice as pets, one soon learns that in spite of docile appearances they can nip a good piece from one's finger and jump quick as a flash in making an escape.

* * * * * * * * * *

The tunnels of moles are often obvious by the broken ridge of earth above them. As far as trapping goes they are the most difficult of small mammals. I knew of one tunnel that, though often crunched in where it crossed a path, had been in use for 20 years. Set a trap by such a runway and the mole will invariably dig under or around it, refusing to get caught.

I was excited one spring to find two Hairytail Moles under an old board in New Hampshire. As they scurried in opposite directions I grabbed one by a hind leg. Getting out the big glass aquarium that I had used for the redback mice I filled the bottom with moist earth. The mole pushed through this as rapidly as a fish through water, using his powerful shoulders and broad front feet.

His activity was unceasing when hungry. If I placed an earthworm on top of the earth, he would locate it from below and pull it down under. A small handful of worms or night crawlers thrown in twice a day kept him content. He got along at other times on meat scraps. He ate mice when I could get them, starting at the head and leaving nothing but skin and tails when finished.

It was fun to watch him move slowly along a tunnel next to the glass, examining every square centimeter of the way with sensitive nose and feet. Sometimes he would pause to push his nose upward and wave it above ground.

* * * * * * * * *

Shrews are seemingly, at times, the most numerous of all small mammals. One June in New Hampshire I caught almost nothing but shorttail shrews regardless of whether I set traps in woods, fields, marshes or even on a mountain top.

These shrews have dark grey fur, sharp noses and tiny black eyes. To catch them alive one must visit traps every few hours for otherwise they are likely to die trying to escape.

I put four shorttails in the big glass aquarium giving each an old sheep's skull to hide in. Without these hide-outs, they would run around until they dropped dead or got into savage fights, severely lacerating one another within a short time.

Shorttail shrews are peculiarly active little creatures, on the go day and night, scooting along runways in field and woodland after insects, worms, baby mice or whatever else falls in their path. I noticed in the aquarium that their long flexible noses, always a-quiver, were the most active part of them. If two shorttails met head-on in a runway, they jumped apart as if touched by an electric shock.

They seemed not at all afraid of us, for I was sometimes able to stroke one with a finger.

Our shrews ate voraciously of fish or animal matter—head, entrails and all. I found by a rather direct method that each shrew ate approximately its own weight in a day, for when one shrew killed another, it had no qualms about eating its victim. One had to be careful.

Shorttail shrews secrete a poison in their saliva that will inactive small prey. It may cause pain to man, but I have been bitten without adverse effect.

Other things noted about our shrews were that they could jump about four inches in spite of their short legs and swim nicely, given water. Most remarkable was something I had never suspected. A shrew would sometimes burst into song. The song was full of chatters, sputters, and other notes, a little suggestive of a red squirrel.

* * * * * * * * * *

One morning when I looked in our menagerie in the barn, every cage was wrecked and empty. A turtle, some frogs, redback mice and all the shrews but one, that had hidden in the cranial cavity of its sheep's skull, were gone. Even the little box traps set out along the wall were torn apart.

In the evening I set out some bait by a pan of fine, smooth mud. The following morning I had some fine imprints of the culprit; a raccoon.

After another week of baiting, the raccoon got enough courage to feed from my hand, even bringing her four young ones with her (See chapter on "Watching Mammals"). As shrews are said to be disdained by most carnivores due to some bad taste or smell, I offered the raccoon a shrew to find out. She gobbled it up without effort. Our pet skunk Jimmy, however, refused to eat a least shrew that it had spent over an hour trying to catch. A pet Great Horned Owl, on the other hand, swallowed the shrew as readily as any other tidbit. There is no accounting for tastes among wild creatures.

The mice, moles and shrews Jane and I kept were but samples of the tremendous populations of gnomes living under dead leaves and grass, stumps and rocks. Without catching them by trap or otherwise, one has little chance of seeing them. It was only by keeping them as captives for a few days that we had opportunities of learning about their lives.

IX. BEAVER AND WILDLIFE

"The animal behavior I have studied–is not physiologically, neurologically, or psychologically slanted so much as ecologically.

The interplay between animals, their behavior and the complexity of their total environment is immensely stimulating."–F. Fraser Darling.

Beaver invaded the southern part of the White Mountains of New Hampshire during World War II years, building dams where none had existed since colonial times. It was a pleasure to see marshes, ponds and swamps enlarging where they had been growing in for years. Beaver are well equipped for this work whether in streams, brooklets and or in established ponds. They are one of the largest of rodents and can scoop loads of mud onto a dam. Like House Wrens, they have a frantic urge to build: one dam succeeding another as they become established along a stream.

Jackmond Pond at Tamworth illustrated how beaver can transform a body of water into a wildlife haven. The pond had diminished in size for years as vegetation from the shore invaded shallow places. This vegetation became a floating mass of sphagnum and sedges in which grew cranberry, pitcher plants, sundew, sweet gale and leather-leaf. In times alders and red maples advanced from the woodland. Breeding ducks found the pond unattractive.

When beaver built dams across the outlet they nearly doubled the area of the pond. Numbers of trees succumbed to the high water. Decaying trunks of white pine, tamarack and red maple became a forest of deed trees standing in water three to five feet deep.

One morning as I paddled my kayak in this bayou I saw a raccoon squatting close to a log. From deeper in I heard the quacking of Black Ducks and the resounding "ker-splash" of a beaver tail hitting the water—a familiar association of sounds, for beaver ponds are often duck ponds as well.

Paddling through the woods was rough on the kayak and I waded into the inner sections of the bayou. My sloshing frightened the ducks but seemed to attract the beaver. One swam to within ten feet, blowing a loud "whew" as he humped, then whacked the water with a resounding "ker-splash". This performance did not seem to indicate alarm for the beaver continued to browse on green plants right afterward. When I scared several deer they bounded away, splashing as they went.

Duck feathers floating on the surface indicated the presence of waterfoul. Black Ducks enjoyed this combination of water and woodland. On some mornings I saw them flying in to seek shelter. On others Black Ducklings scooted over the surface to disappear between tree trunks. One June evening nine Wood Duck arose from the bayou, circled against the mountains, then perched on a large pine.

I once saw what I thought was a Wood Duck fly through the trees and alight at the top of a dead tamarack 50 or more feet above the water. But it was, I found, a female Hooded Merganser searching for a nest hole. For several summers a lone Canada Goose visited the pond although no one had kept decoys in the vicinity.

The bayou attracted many types of birds besides ducks. In addition to Green and Great Blue herons, Red-wings and grackles, there were others that like dead trees to nest in. These included Bluebirds, Tree Swallows, Crested Flycatchers, Hairy Woodpeckers, and flickers. But the song that dominated the bayou was that of the Northern Waterthrush.

Seeking its nest, I studied stumps of overturned trees. A Waterthrush flew as I neared the second one, pretending to have broken a wing—an act difficult to perform over open water. The nest was a cup of moss lined with deer hair. The beaver, that had provided the waterthrush with its flooded stump, had also attracted the deer that supplied the lining for its nest.

Beaver usually build a single dam sufficient when across slower streams to create a long, narrow pond. But in the more rapid water of mountain valleys they have to build a succession of dams to compensate for the short back up from any one.

The type of fish thriving in beaver ponds depends upon a number of factors. Trout prefer cooler, well-aerated water, a condition beaver may destroy by exposing more surface to the sun and slowing the current. Perch then supplant trout in the warmer ponds. Frogs and tadpoles, preyed upon by many animals, find a variety of conditions suitable.

Beaver can effect marked changes when they dam small brooklets. I know of one brooklet where a beaver dam several hundred feet long and containing much mud scooped from the bottom, transformed an old pasture into a small lake. Here, on a quiet evening when its surface reflected the mountains and trout leapt for flies, one might see a beaver as it swam out from its lodge by the shore. Above the lake, in a chain of successively smaller ponds, I sometimes startled a Black Duck or a Wood Duck with her brood. All this in a worn-out pasture!

On another occasion I searched the foot of Flat Mountain for a beaver pond that I knew lay hidden below a steep slope. As I pushed through the woods I heard Black Ducks quacking. It was this that led me to the pond with its beaver lodge. Two Black Ducks sprang up. One flew off over the trees. The other—the mother—flopped back to the water with an injured wing, floundering about while her six ducklings scrambled for shelter.

I had an unexpected piece of good fortune by this beaver pond. In the low growth of canoe birch and aspens along the shore I heard then saw a pair of Philadelphia Vireos that were apparently nesting in the vicinity.

Thus as beaver have increased in New Hampshire, conditions for wildlife have improved. Yet many consider the beaver a pest. Of what use, they ask, is an animal that floods an occasional road, field or woodlot? Complaints against beaver keep game wardens busy. Breaking a dam is of little avail, so quickly is it repaired, and catching beaver in box traps for deportation is not easy.

Beavers do little damage by felling trees because most of the ones they feed on—such as alder, aspens, grey birch and wild cherry—are of small value. True, they occasionally destroy valuable timber by inundation. But are there any wild mammals, from deer to chipmunks, that do not in some way conflict with man, himself the greatest destroyer of all?

One wishes that the harmful aspects of beaver might be balanced against the constructive. Beaver dams conserve water and in so doing help prevent forest fires, floods and soil erosion. Their ponds and swamps furnish refuges for many types of wildlife. Above all, the beaver is one of the most interesting of animals. His enterprise and community developments can be seen by almost anyone who is interested, sometimes close to main highways. Were he more fully understood and appreciated, the beaver might be better tolerated by his human neighbors, at least in New England.

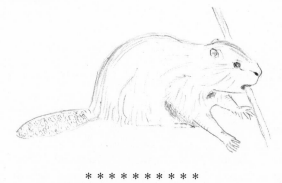

* * * * * * * * * *

When a conservation officer dynamited a beaver dam near our home one June, in response to the request of a land-owner, something miraculous happened. Floating on the water after the explosion was a tiny beaver unharmed and apparently born not long before. The officer, knowing of our love of raising wild animals, brought it to us.

Bev, as we called our pint-sized beaver, was affectionate from the start. We placed her in a large aquarium atop a wood stove in the kitchen. Here anyone wanting to take out the cuddly animal and feed it its bottle could do so.

Bev soon graduated to a diet of Purina Dog Chow and other artificial food. I had thought it would be more natural, as well as cheaper, to feed her sections from limbs and trunks of aspens, but Bev was adamant: she preferred packaged foods. She did, none the less, gnaw logs of wood as a way of exercising her ever-growing incisors.

These huge, orange-colored teeth were formidable. Beaver can fell large trees. But Bev remained a docile, harmless, affectionate creature. She never tried to bite us nor, thankfully, to gnaw furniture or woodwork when loose in the house.

Bev liked to be lifted out of her aquarium, especially in the evening. But she objected to being held, expressing her desire to reach the floor by flailing her tail up and down. She had work to do.

The work followed much the same pattern every evening. Bev regarded the kitchen as a pond and the doors as outlets to be dammed. Brushes, a dust pan, sticks of stove wood, old dish cloths, and anything she could find were dragged to these strategic spots. She often upset the dog's water dish on the way, giving her pond a touch of reality.

Sometimes we returned to the kitchen to find that Bev had disappeared. Where could she have gone in our large 1812 house? Once discovered, we found that she always went to the same place. This was the linen closet on the second floor. Bev negotiated the stairs readily when seeking this cozy place that to her, no doubt, was a beaver lodge de luxe.

When gathered in one's arms and carried downstairs, tail thrashing all of the way, Bev settled back in her aquarium to eat, rest, or gnaw. She was a most contented creature.

How could a beaver approaching adult size be content to live in an aquarium? I think this was because she regarded it as the inner chamber of a lodge, probably as large as beaver occupy naturally.

After months of lifting Bev about, in addition to other house work, Jane began to find Bev's increasing weight and strength hard to manage, especially the big thrashing tail. What could be a solution?

A solution, fortunately, was not long in coming. A doctor in Vermont who had raised a male beaver of the same age as Bev, wanted a mate for it. He had a small pond. All he needed was a pair. The situation was ideal and we took Bev over.

I do not know what Bev was thinking when she swam away from us, but possibly she was gasping: "Gee, this is the best kitchen I have seen yet."

We were sorry to see Bev go. I had a feeling from seeing how warm and friendly she had been with us that beaver must be lovable when among their own kind; a thought that comes to me when I watch beaver in the wild.

X. THE POND AND CATTAILS

"In paths untrodden,
In the growth by margins of pond waters."–Walt Whitman.

I have always loved ponds—not so much clear, deep ones lined by rocks and sand as marshy ones, choked in places with aquatic vegetation, where all kinds of creatures might lurk and be found if one took the time. Yet almost never have there been such ponds near where Jane or I have lived or traveled to study birds.

Now here on Sapelo was one at last: I wanted to sit and watch it, no matter how little might happen—to develop the art of being a pond-watcher as one might develop the art of watching by a nest. The approach is similar.

Only by observing, recording, then later reliving one's experiences by writing one can hope to acquire any art involving natural history. Or so I feel. My experiments in pond-watching began slowly, gathering momentum as they went along.

19 March

As I walk along the causeway, I pause to look through a gap in the hedge to watch a coot moving against the reeds. Then I see the necks of a pair of

Blue-winged Teal resting at the fringe of marsh vegetation, their heads up in semi-alert. A Pied-billed
Grebe swims close in front of them and behind I have
a glimpse, frustratingly brief, of a Sora in the jungle
of reeds. What a beautiful exhibit of marsh life, all
neatly framed by one small gap in the bushes.

21 March

Today I bring my bird chair where I can look
through the hedge without being seen.

There is always life on the pond. At the corner
opposite a dozen Snowy Egrets are perched in several
small trees, resting in the sun. One occasionally raises
its crest and displays its plumes.

The pond is flat and calm. A swarm of Tree Swal-
los, white bellies flashing in the sun, fly back and
forth over it. Otherwise, the same scaup, Common
Gallinule, coots and Blue-winged Teal are here as on
other days.

One new bird I am to see on the pond only once is
an Anhinga. It glides by in fine view, its spear-like bill
leading the way. The anhinga has grey silky feathers
against the dark background of upper wings.

22 March

Things of Beauty Recalled:
The Blue-winged Teal in the shallow, marshy end
of the pond, feeding on duck-weed. The exquisite
beauty of plumages in the morning sun.

Three male Boat-tailed Grackles in a bare place in
the brackish marsh, tails and heads up, walking with
widely spaced legs . . . a wonderful sheen to their
feathers.

A Louisiana Heron standing at the edge of the reeds by the pond edge, its white belly looking like a white vest, its grey wings like a coat.

23 March

On a visit at mid-morning the pond is still enveloped by sea mist. Diagonally across from a break in the bushes I make out the head and back of the large alligator, the only big one in the pond. It lies lazily like

a floating log. When I come to the water's edge, it submerges with only the tip of snout and eyes protruding. As I wait his back reappears. What does this huge creature feed on—ducks, fish, herons?

On another visit I work my way through the hedge, carefully breaking dead branches until I have a place where I can sit and watch while remaining hidden. My settling frightens a Louisiana Heron but a pair of coot, close to against a background of reeds, remain undisturbed. They dabble at vegetation or stand on their heads to pull food from the bottom, rarely going completely under. I never tire of studying details. The white bills of the coot are set off by their woolly black necks and chunky grey bodies.

The quiet of the marsh suddenly explodes with the loud, rapid "hn, hn, hn" of a Pied-billed Grebe hidden from view but obviously close by. It takes some moments to find for, with body submerged, only its head and neck show above water. When it finally bobs up its plumage, unlike that of coot and teal, looks as wet as that of a swimming muskrat. I now have a view of the black ring around its bill, the white eye-ring and the black patch below the chin. The grebe has a fierce look as it swings as though at anchor.

I have my thrill of the morning where cattails come close. Just inside the green wall is an opening formed by a mat of dead cattails. Walking onto the open place are two Soras their bills yellow in the sunshine and not 15 feet from where I sit. After a few moments they disappear into the jungle of cattails where they are usually impossible to see.

Hundreds of tree swallows move almost of one accord as they fly close over the water, rise, and turn with a flash of white bellies to come over the water again.

24 March

I work my folding chair out onto a small peninsula that juts into the shallow upper part of the pond. Several dozen Blue-winged Teal feed among the thinly scattered reeds, all in pairs and mostly bottoms up. Among them is a Common Gallinule, its frontal shield and bill a bright, gleaming red as it dabs here and there while swimming directly toward me. When it reaches a patch of cress-like, leafy plants, it plucks and eats them rapidly.

Strange to think that this same bird, known as the Moorhen, is common in England. It is far more conspicuous there than with us, running about open spaces and pastures along streams.

25 March

Louisiana Herons are the most wary of the marsh birds. While I can usually get into my hideouts and sit down without scaring coot, teal, or gallinule, the single Louisiana Heron that is often among them flies away with loud "cawk, cawks."

But I am becoming more skillful. This morning I see the heron moving belly-deep in the water, its grey body and neck slightly obscured by a screen of reeds. Everything shows well in the sunlight: the white of its thighs, of its throat (no more than a band down the center), the white trim of its shoulders and the white

plume hanging down from the back of its head. The
heron seems undisturbed by my watching. Its head,
neck and long bill reach forward like a spear. Then
there is a quick jab as some aquatic organism is seized
at or close to the surface.

A fascination of heron-watching is the variety of
poses the long legs, necks, and bills allow them to
assume.

I make a second visit to the pond in the late afternoon when the sun is behind me. One coot is preening, another splashing with its wings as it takes a bath.
Blue-winged Teal, in spite of their constant
bottoms-up in feeding, have feathers that form one
impervious, varnished cover that gleams when it
catches the sun.

Do they feed all day and not at night? About ten on
the pond rest with heads tucked back in wings.

26 March

Jane was disconsolate yesterday at having seen a
rail not pictured in Peterson's Field Guide. As I always find the birds I am looking for in his book, I was
able to give little help.

Today as I sit in the best of my rail hideouts I find
Jane's bird on a mat of dead cattails. It is obviously
half-way in moulting from a juvenile to an adult Sora.
Its head colors—rufous on crown, grey on cheeks,
small white spot just behind the eye—remind me of a
male House Sparrow, as does the dark on the throat.

The same Sora with the House Sparrow look flies
across a small stretch of water to enter the cattails
when I return in the late afternoon. The low rays of
the sun slant into the jungle of stalks, giving views of
the Sora picking its way about on floating vegetation.

Walking out on a submerged, rotting stalk, it pecks rapidly to right and left on prey too minute to see. The farther the rail emerges the more the dead stalk sinks: the rail is soon in water up to its belly.

27 March

On this second day of cold north winds five Blue-winged Teal sleep at mid-morning, heads tucked in wings as their bodies sway in the water like boats at anchor in a harbor. Two thick bunches of reeds protect them from the wind.

I especially enjoy watching a Pied-billed Grebe, feathers fluffed as it rides high and lightly on the surface, resting and stretching. With each stretch a short wing extends backward, covering the grebe's rear end as the leg of the same side, stretched at the same time, extends backward. The leg, in returning, takes a longer time to get back in place than the wing. The grebe also scratches its head.

Is the effect of the wind to make teal and grebe do more resting than usual? These little grebes have a penetrating gaze. No other marsh birds look at me so directly.

28 March

A commotion as one Pied-bill shoots out of the cattails in pursuit of another. Both sink from sight when they reach open water. One, a handsome individual in breeding plumage, bobs up looking, I think, rather pleased with himself. With a sudden stir of water the second grebe rams him from below. I never see the second grebe emerge. The first bird sinks directly downward following the attack—no leaping forward as in a usual dive. It is miraculous the way grebes can disappear.

29 March

The pond lies quietly in the late afternoon sun. A few Ring-billed Gulls circle the open water in easy flight and a male Lesser Scaup ventures farther than usual into the little bay by my hideout. A Snowy Egret flies to the muddy point at the end of the cattails. It must have seen something from a distance for it jabs repeatedly with its slender black bill before flying off.

I look again at the scaup; the beautiful black of head, neck and breast, the blue bill and gleaming white flanks below its greyish back. There is nothing like an afternoon sun behind one for seeing colors.

These watchings divert me from a Sora close by and in the open. What exquisite plumage on its back—rich brown feathers with margins of white. The rail moves along slowly, making innumerable jabs to right, left and front as it goes over each projecting bit of water-weed. Whatever it is feeding on seems very tiny for a bird roughly the size of a robin.

Male Boat-tailed Grackles are coming to the cattails increasingly. They fly with a curiously heavy sound. On windy days their long tails appear to be no asset, serving only to slew them around. What beauties these birds are in the sun with blue irridescence over breast and wings, black on the head and bright yellow eyes.

30 March

Just in front of where I sit is a small bay with a wall of cattails along the end and farther side. I call it Quiberon Bay because of the naval battles taking place there—battles not between British and French men-of-war but between two Pied-billed Grebes.

This morning I see another engagement. At first the two belligerents, one an adult and the other in nondescript plumage, are floating six feet apart. One dives, coming up to ram the other from below. The two now face each other several feet apart, heads drawn back, necks S-shaped and gular pouches inflated, giving a heavy look to throat and cheeks.

Then both submerge, perhaps to carry on submarine warfare. Will they surface somewhere among the cattails? These grebes have a way of leaving one with many questions.

* * * * * * * * * *

Coming back along the causeway as the sun emerges from mists I see 19 Snowy Egrets and one Louisiana Heron perched at varying heights among the low trees at the north end of the pond.

There is a small duck-weed-covered opening among the cattails where two coot always skitter away in alarm when I pass. Yet today when I sit boldly at the edge of their domain, they continue to feed undisturbed.

Possibly they are in the midst of other concerns. One coot approaches the other, head and neck low

and lower mandible down; then seizes its companion
by the neck, only, in turn, to be seized in similar fashion. After this brief exchange, the two continue feeding as before.

This is a morning of conflicts. Two Common Gallinules clash back in the reeds, then churn out into
open water. I now perceive that the loud array of
"kud-ders" and "cowps" I have heard issuing from
the depths of the cattails come from the gallinules.
One swims away from the other with the white
patches of its tail fanned.

A third conflict of the morning occurs just as I
leave the pond and look up to see three Red-tailed
Hawks sailing over the salt marsh. One drops down
on the other, talons extended. The two nearly grapple, then separate. All three continue circling until
they disappear over the pine trees.

Conflict or courtship? I am not sure.

* * * * * * * * *

When a Louisiana Heron flies it makes crow-like
"cawk, cawks" or "cracks", drawn out in a lugubrious
way. I thought at first they only did this when
frightened. But yesterday one came gliding in over
the pond to alight in the cattails, making the notes
when apparently undisturbed.

I slip into my hideout this mild and misty morning
without disturbing a Louisiana Heron standing at attention against a background of reeds. No stalking of
prey as a few days ago: the heron stands waiting, neck
curved, ready to strike at prey coming within reach.

The heron is not alone. A pair of coot feed sometimes within five, sometimes within only two feet

from where it stands. "Why doesn't the heron move?" I query. "Will not the dabbling and turmoil of the coot drive away small fish and other prey?" But the heron appears content where it is. Within a short period the heron poises itself, then makes a lightening stab as it moves ahead a few steps, only to return to its original position.

It then occurs to me that the coot are probably aiding the heron by flushing tadpoles, fish or other organisms out into the open where the heron can seize them. The prey seized is sizeable, but I cannot identify it for certain. One small fish is held momentarily at the bill tip. The heron tosses the fish back into his gullet with a quick, deft motion, then returns to his sentrylike pose by the tuft of reeds.

The coot are certainly no hindrance. When they leave the heron still catches prey, although I think not quite as well as before. It would take many timings and countings to find this out exactly. Sometimes the heron, with head and neck held low and foward, takes three or four strides before striking. It has a fan of plumes coming down over its back, largely covering its wings, whenever it resumes its position of standing and waiting.

Why should a Louisiana Heron stick to one method of fishing one day and use an alternate method—slow stalking—on another? This may have something to do with the sun and the glare on the water. Possibly this misty morning, with an absence of glare, is favorable to the motionless waiting. The visibility is equally good in all directions.

1 April

Boat-tailed Grackles are always amusing to watch. In the stretch of black mud left where waters have

receded from lack of rain, a female grackle in brown
plumage (she does not have the boat tail of the male)
comes repeatedly to gather mud and soggy bits of
dead reeds. She then flies her nest material up over
the cattails, only to plunk down among them shortly
beyond. A male meanwhile comes to a bush nearby
that he uses for perching morning after morning.

Another grackle now comes flying in across the
pond holding a long streamer of grass in her bill. She
is escorted by a second male. Both sexes make heavy
wing noises in flight.

* * * * * * * * * *

I saw some amusing performances in the evening
in a pine tree well away from the pond. A heavy flutter noise as of wings, a curious sound that continued,
led me to look up. A female grackle, sitting as still as
the tossing of the pine in a mild breeze allowed, was
perched at the top. A male below was courting her
most intensively; head-feathers ruffed, beak opened
half an inch and head bent down in exaggerated fashion. He kept fluttering his partly opened wings. She
remained looking straight ahead, seemingly unin-
terested. The male kept his head bent down and away
from her but turned, at times, to face her with an
open bill. These performances went on for five minutes.

I had seen none of them among the cattails where the females were nest building. Is the courting of these birds carried on away from nest sites?

3 April

I have not seen the 'gator for several days in his usual place where he floats in open water. I have doubtless been looking in the wrong place.

This morning I discover his sunning place on the far bank and see his whole length for the first time! He is a massive relic from the age of the dinosaurs. When I try to point him out to Jane, he takes alarm and slides into the water.

* * * * * * * * *

Although I have had few opportunities for pond-watching in the south other than Sapelo, I once spent hours watching Pied-billed Grebes on a small pond by the Potomac. It was a beautiful morning, with red-bud and dogwood coming into bloom. Grebes are my favorites in marshy ponds and on this and following days I saw some curious bits of behavior.

What was possibly a male submerged when about 20 feet from a female Ring-necked Duck, then delivered a swift attack, ramming the duck from below. Once the duck had been driven away the grebe burst into a loud "ka, ka, cow, cow", swelling and collapsing the sides of his neck as he did so.

Why should the grebe have attacked the duck? And why just one species, for the grebe did not attack Wood Duck or Blue-winged Teal.

After I had watched a number of attacks I realized that a female Ring-necked Duck has markings similar to those of Pied-billed Grebes. Each has a ring around the bill; a way of diving that exposes a white belly and similar body size. All of these—or some of them— presumably acted as signals or "releasers" of territorial behavior in the grebe that attacked the duck as if it were a rival of its own kind. This idea was reinforced on several occasions when the grebe attacked an imma- ture of its own species in the same manner.

Another bit of behavior fascinating to me occurred on the 28th of March when two grebe swam together and touched bills as one made a rapid "h'n, h'n" noise resembling a nasal laugh.

On 12 April I saw another kind of courtship. One of the grebes had remained motionless when it sud- denly stood upright on the surface beating its wings and treading water with both feet, yet remaining in the same spot. A second grebe was 20 feet away. In a few moments the two swam together and, with much splashing followed by submergence, they attempted to mate.

My observations led me to read a paper written by Sir Julian Huxley in 1914. It is a classic on the court- ship of the Great Crested, a common and spectacular grebe of marshy ponds in Europe.

"I hope," wrote Huxley about his paper, that it will "help to show what a wealth of interesting things still lie hidden in and about the breeding places of familiar birds. A good glass, a notebook, some patience and a spare fortnight in the spring—with these I not only managed to discover unknown facts about the Crested Grebe, but also had one of the pleasantest of holidays."

Huxley did more than discover a few facts. He brought out that the grebes, like many other birds, do not take their pair bonds for granted. They renew them with little ceremonies many times a day, even if these amount to no more than one offering the other a bit of pond weed.

While I never offered Jane anything as tangible on our Sapelo days, I like to think that experiences shared, for she also spent many happy hours watching by the pond, were something of a substitute.

XI. WATCHING SNAKES WITH A BIRD GLASS

"You road I enter upon and look around, I believe you are not all that is here.
I believe that much unseen is also here."–Walt Whitman.

The causeway that ran by the pond to the beach made a beautiful walk. On days of blue sky and white clouds, it was difficult to keep the eye from vistas of salt marsh, sand dunes, and woodland borders. Yet with the first days of spring I wanted to become a snake watcher and this meant keeping an eye to the ground as I went from place to place.

Why snakes with so much else to look for? I have had a delight in snakes and reptiles from earliest years but it never throve, living as I have in New Hampshire.

A glorious southern spring such as we are enjoying on Sapelo Island served to awaken interests long dormant. The causeway was the place to begin. It ran from a Pileated Woodpecker nest in a huge dead pine at one end, to the beach at the other. It was a walk Jane and I often took, as Robert Frost would have it, for "change of solitude . . ." the solitude of a turn by the nest to one of watching by pond or sea.

The causeway, running between fresh water ditches with lagoons on one side and a pond with cattails on the other, was especially favorable for snakes. It was a place where snakes crossed as well as one where they could lie in the sun, torpid from winter inactivity. Some of the causeway ran past brackish marsh and some through pines. There was thus a variety of habitat with bushes giving shelter on either side.

The torpidity of the snakes permitted close views. My first encounter was with a mole snake about two feet long. It remained so motionless that I lay down to look within inches at its smooth, shiny, varnished-like brown scales, shading to yellowish near the belly. Although its body lay still, the dark, limpid eyes moved about as alertly as those of a lizard.

There was a time when I used to capture snakes, partly to see if I could be quick and skillful enough to do so. It was not always easy. At other times it was to bring them home, keep them for a few days of taking pictures, then to release them. But capturing a snake is a traumatic experience. If one presses down with a foot or forked stick the creature, badly frightened, thrashes about to escape and may injure itself. Then when handled, some, such as water and garter snakes, try to bite while giving off an offensive odor.

I was ready for a new approach on Sapelo. I wanted to enjoy snakes in natural surroundings and to enjoy them peacefully. From this point of view my encounter with the mole snake, eye-to-eye at ground level, was most satisfying.

Several days later rain flooded some deep ruts in the causeway. As I was skirting one of these I noticed a snake about two and a half feet long trying to conceal itself in black mud at the bottom. This was one I would have to disturb if I was to see it at all. I inserted a stick under it ever-so-gently for a look at its banded pattern. A glance at its head showed that it was not a cottonmouth but rather a banded water snake, much like ones I had handled in New Hampshire. The rain had seemingly led it to travel over wet terrain, probably in pursuit of frogs.

As days went by I learned that sun, rains at night and a day neither too hot nor too cool make for good snaking in early spring.

By these standards the 24th of March was a fine day. Jane and I were taking our usual turns at the Pileated nest. On my first walk out along the causeway I met a mud turtle and a king snake at the same time, both wet from a nearby ditch. The king snake was particularly handsome; the jet black with white of its four-foot body gleaming in the sunlight as it made its way into the woods.

After a second tour at the nest I noticed what appeared to be a reticulated stick lying across the pine needles. I lifted my glasses for a look. To my joy I had come across a diamondback rattlesnake—sluggish and small but our first at Sapelo. I got between it and the woods and called for Jane.

Our rattler was a docile, inoffensive one, showing no disposition to strike. Jane tried some sketches. While admiring the snake's beauty of color and pattern I particularly noted the black patch sweeping back from the eye.

As Jane continued her work I wondered why some animals, as widely separated as wood frogs, diamondback rattlers and raccoons, have black masks. Does it have to do with being night hunters? Is it a way of concealing their eyes?

With the young diamondback, as with several monarch butterflies seen along the causeway, the image of beauty lingered. What wonderful patterns, designs! What miracles nature has performed with its natural selection of color through the eons of time!

On returning to the beach in the afternoon I had a view of a black snake with a white chin as it moved slowly through the bushes. It was a black racer, head raised and tongue darting. I watched several of these snakes hunting later on: the first one raised its head perhaps eight inches to look around, paying little regard to me. Then it progressed through the short grass, pausing to investigate small leaves and blades with a flickering tongue. Was it on the trail of a mate? Or was it sensing traces of prey?

A difficulty with most snakes is that one cannot follow them long enough. They get swallowed up in vegetation. If only I could see one stalk and capture prey!

The nearest I came to this was on March 31. I was walking along the muddy shore of the pond, close to the causeway—which was actually a dike enclosing it—when I glimpsed a most unusual sight. Had I not been looking for a Sora that I suspected was just ahead, and hopefully for the alligator that sunned itself on a bank opposite, I might have seen the black snake at my feet sooner. As it was, I saw the racer dragging another snake by the neck and about to enter some bushes.

Reverting to the habit I was trying to break, I did a foolish thing. I made a quick grab. The racer dropped its prey and left. The victim was a mole snake, benumbed and barely alive. How could it have been injured so severely? There were a series of bites from tail to head where the black snake had clamped its jaws, leaving little tooth marks. But a black snake's teeth are tiny. How could they seriously injure a snake two feet long and half its own size? Does the saliva of black snakes have some narcotizing effect?

I have been bitten, harmlessly, by black snakes that struck at my bare legs. Might repeated bites on a small victim add up differently? King snakes kill other snakes by coiling and squeezing. Racers have no such abilities.

The only other snake we found along the causeway was a large rat snake draped over low bushes in the sun and undisturbed by our standing eight feet away to watch and sketch.

* * * * * * * * *

It was now getting time for us to leave the island. Due to the earliness of the season we had seen a number of fine snakes, such as the rat snake, under excellent condition. But on rainy days I felt that I missed many.

One has to be alert to be a snake watcher. Sometimes by blundering along too fast, all I saw was a tail disappearing in the bushes. To become a good snake watcher, I decided, would take time. I would have to think snakes if I was to see them before I got too close.

For a moment I fancied Jane being asked what we did on Sapelo. She would tell friends that I saw snakes. Eye-brows would be raised. "Seeing snakes?" *Delirium tremens?*—her husband a victim, no doubt, of southern moonshine.

I am convinced, nonetheless, that starting a new kind of watching takes patience as well as a habit of thinking and seeing. But then what is more intoxicating than finding new sources of beauty in nature, new fields for discovery?

"How much," wrote Thoreau, "what infinite leisure it requires, as of a lifetime, to appreciate a single phenomenon! You camp down beside it as for life, having reached your land of promise, and give yourself wholly to it. It must stand for the whole world to you, symbolical of all things."

SOUTH CAROLINA PLANTATION

The plantation was a large one, 23,000 acres along the Savannah River. I followed the car ahead carefully over mile after mile of narrow sandy road, streamers of Spanish moss catching the windshield from low-growing branches.

The Groton Plantation was everywhere much the same; ground still blackened by the annual spring burning; thinned out groves of pines and oaks favorable for quail shooting; the occasional plowed field rented to farmers for planting corn. Ditches and low places were full of water.

At last we approached what was to be our camp. The plantation manager's wife stepped from the car

ahead, somewhat apologetic. The camp was no more
than a galvanized-iron-sheeting affair with outdoor
tables and a stove, set on a cement platform, without
screens and much open to the breezes.

She obviously had had to spend some time cleaning
out accumulations left by hunters in the fall.

There was no need for apologies. The shack had a
pleasant, well-settled look in its grove of pines and
oaks streaming with Spanish moss. In front was an
old-fashioned pump for water; inside a stove, a fireplace, and two comfortable cots. Jane and I would fare
well.

How pleasant to be able to eat with views out
through the woods, yet with a tight roof in case of
rain! The older such a shack becomes, the more nature creeps in. Jane and I were grateful.

Once we had made a start at unloading our gear, I
began making forays into the surrounding bush. The
shack was to be our home for a few weeks. What
birds, snakes, or other creatures lived close by?

First explorations around a new camp are always exciting for a naturalist. I had gone hardly 50 feet before finding a five-foot king snake stretched out on a harrowed strip. It remained where it was, even after I had called to Jane to come have a look.

A half hour later I led Jane along the same dirt roadway to show her an old nest of a Pileated Woodpecker. We had progressed only a short distance when we saw a strange snake lying in the dirt ahead of us. Like other snakes we encountered on our first day this one seemed indifferent to close approach.

What an odd-looking creature! What could it be? It was only two feet long but had a disproportionately wide head, light tan in color, with two large black spots. Behind these was a bulge of some just-swallowed prey. Possibly the meal made the snake sluggish for it moved only slowly along its way.

We walked close and examined all details with our bird glasses. The snake had two pits on its head, one on either side—a pit viper. One difficulty in making a diagnosis was that the black tail was stumpy, as though bitten off. Conant's Field Guide, however, made it clear that this was a canebrake rattler, even though its rattles were missing . . . the first such rattler Jane and I had ever seen. A camp with rattle-snakes close by! Prospects looked good indeed for my new hobby of snakewatching.

A half hour later, in the heat of mid-day, I was ready for another exploration of terrain near Tuten's Plaza, to use the elegant name tacked above our camp.

Having just read Carl Kauffeld's "Snakes and Snake Hunting," much of which was written about this same South Carolina country, I became interested in a pile of rotting railroad ties 40 feet away. It might be an ideal place. After inspecting one side of the pile and seeing nothing, I was about to step across to the other when I hesitated. Maybe I had better take a close look. It was just as well I did. There, right where I would have put my foot, was a magnificent canebrake rattler over three feet long.

A pleasant feature of looking through a bird glass is that it makes things look larger. The snake thus looked about four-and-a-half feet long and as thick around as my forearm—a fine healthy specimen. Unlike our first canebrake of the morning, this one had a tail with eight rattles. I called Jane to bring her sketch pad. She made several sketches while I stood taking in every detail of my find. We immediately named him Canebrake.

It was marvelous the way the snake, sunning himself in the open, was camouflaged against a background of matted oak leaves. He did not move. Kauffeld calls the canebrake the "monarch of the swamp". Of one he found stretched out in a patch of sunlight, much as ours was, he wrote that the setting "made such a picture as to give me exquisite pleasure. I do not know how long I stood motionless, drinking in every detail to impress it indelibly on my memory. No camera can capture scenes such as this—I like my memory pictures much better."

* * * * * * * * * *

It was Jane who found our third snake. She was taking a stroll when she came to a place where the

small dirt road ran between two swampy places. Here a cottonmouth, coiled at the water edge, displayed at her with mouth wide open. When I came by 20 minutes later it was still in the same place, but instead of opening its mouth, the snake lay still, long enough for me to have a close look at its dark brown body and black stripe extending from the eye. It then moved slowly into the water.

Our fourth and last snake of the day was a garter snake, found as it was about to cross an open space when the air had become cool in the afternoon. Unlike any other garter snake I have seen, this one lacked the usual yellow strips, having only black spots on his uniformly brown back.

Four kinds of snakes, two of them poisonous and all ones well seen, was, I felt, a good start for our hunter's camp.

One of the things I most loved about Tuten's Plaza was being able to step directly out into the darkness at night. Such forays are one of the joys of camping out and some of my strongest impressions of South Carolina were of taking only ten to 15 steps under the pines.

The night of our arrival, April 27, was clear and cool. The dark sky, as seen through the pine branches, was studded with bright stars. Of the same size as the stars, and seeming extensions of them, were fireflies flashing nearer to us. A weird effect this, stars and fireflies all twinkling and alive against the misty grey setting of Spanish moss; and out beyond, in the further darkness, a chorus of hundreds of frogs all going at once. What an incredible din! How exciting, almost overwhelming nature can be in the southlands!

The great chorus of frogs died away as the moon rose about midnight; only the deep bass of occasional bullfrogs in a small pond continuing. As the night moved on, I made other visits to listen and drink in the beauty of our surroundings, hearing the hootings of Barred Owls and the calls of Chuck-will's-widows. Always as I walked about in the dimness was the thought, will I step on Canebrake? This was a rather scary idea, one that made my senses even more alert to the beauties of the night.

But what was Canebrake doing? Did he sleep by day then roam about hunting by night? I always carried a flash lamp to avoid coming too close or stepping on him. But Canebrake was not moving. Every time I strolled over to swing a beam of light under the old railroad ties, I could see a coil or two of our neighbor as he rested as motionless by night as by day. How long would he stay with us?

Each day when I returned from sessions of watching the Red-headed Woodpeckers we had come to study, I strolled over to the pile of old ties to inspect Canebrake. Our "pet" emerged from his lair each mid-morning, had a long afternoon siesta, then returned to his shelter with equal slowness toward evening.

He was seldom easy to see at a glance. Sometimes when I looked carefully at the bed of dry oak leaves, a

few curled to give dark patches alternating with patches of sunlight, I would say "there he is" only to find, on more prolonged inspection, that he was not at that particular place at all. At other times I would say, "I can't find him, has he left us?" Then gradually I would make out his beautiful pattern, loosely curled, blending perfectly with the background of old leaves and weathered wood. Canebrake had chosen his shelter well.

What a crime to pull aside old planks and logs when searching for snakes or other creatures! How important are all good hideouts. We should leave them intact.

There was, in the case of Canebrake, the beauty and fascination of the creature, and then the beauty of his little bit of selected habitat to which he was so well adapted. When Canebrake lay in loose coils, seemingly asleep in the sun, his head was difficult to see. This was partly because his eyes, no more than vertical slits, were so lifeless. His black tail and rattle in contrast, were easier to distinguish.

The sky clouded over at 5:30 on the afternoon of April 30 as a thunderstorm passed to the south of us. A cool breeze swept through the camp and the swamp frogs began to sing. What effect would the storm have on the rattler? When I walked over for a look I found that Canebrake's head had already disappeared under the old beam that formed his lair. His body followed, then the black tail and rattle. His day was over and his night had begun.

Canebrake came from his shelter at 11:10 the following morning as the sun emerged from mist. It took him until noon to reach his coiling-out place a few feet away.

The growing heat seemed to make him restless. By one o'clock he was partially back under his beam, but an hour later he returned to his bed of leaves where he remained all afternoon. Sometime between 7:00 and 7:15 he flowed under the beam entirely. Thus I kept track of his peregrinations, continuing to keep watch with my torch by night.

I do not believe Canebrake ever moved any distance away from the railroad ties for nine days. It was apparent that although he looked plump and well fed when first found, he was becoming thinner as days and nights wore on.

Meanwhile I was not losing touch with our other neighbor, the cottonmouth. Jane and I found him repeatedly where the dirt road ran between two small stretches of water. When I paid my visit on April 30, I said, "I will keep to the left, as Cottonmouth always lies on the right. I will thus avoid coming too close."

Scanning to the right I almost forgot to look directly in front of me. When I did, Cottonmouth was almost at my feet, his tail lying in the dirt track where I might have stepped on him. He lay on a flat stone above a small culvert, his triangular, potent-looking head resting on his brown, mud colored body. Cottonmouth, like Canebrake, seemingly paid no attention to my proximity. When Jane came to sketch him later, he let her get started, then slithered off into the dark water.

I like what Kauffeld has to say about cottonmouths. "Cottonmouth Moccasins," he wrote, "are admirable in many ways: if a snake can be said to be philosophical, the term could apply to them. Not only do they usually accept captivity goodnaturedly, but in the wild they seem to adjust to a variety of habitats; so long as they are near water they are satisfied, and if circumstances require a change of diet, they seem to take whatever is at hand—ophidian opportunists who take advantage of whatever nature offers. This makes a 'successful' species, and the Moccasins are certainly that."

But cottonmouths are not always peaceful. At another part of the plantation, I was walking a plank that spanned a rain-water creek when a sudden stir made me look down at the muddy water. There, his triangular head drawn back and ready to strike, was a thick-set cottonmouth only eight inches from my foot.

Wherever I moved, he moved to face me in a bold, aggressive way. He could easily have escaped if he had wanted to. When I started to move away the cottonmouth started moving down the creek. When I returned, thinking to watch him slither away, he came right back to coil and coldly and aggressively face me again.

I walked on thinking that this would be the last of the incident. Jane, however, crossing the plank a half-hour later, saw a remarkable sight. As she looked down she saw a snake with large horns making off along the narrow creek. The "horns" were the projecting legs of a frog whose body was already inside the snake's mouth! From Jane's description, it seemed possible that she saw the same cottonmouth that I had encountered.

Like other snakes, cottonmouths can vary in temperament. "Sometimes" wrote Kauffeld, "they are waspishly irritable, taking offense at the lightest disturbance by vibrating the tail rapidly and striking repeatedly at any moving object. Others are phlegmatic and good-natured—nothing seems to arouse them."

I wonder if conditions determine such changes of disposition. If stomachs and digestive tracts are full of prey undergoing slow digestion, snakes are peaceful and indolent. When digestion is completed and they start out again in search of prey, they become alert and irritable. Our cottonmouth by the plank was obviously hunting. It seemed unlikely, otherwise, that it would have left the safety of the swamp that lay close below.

* * * * * * * * *

In watching Canebrake I came to realize that his attraction to the vicinity of Tuten's Plaza may have been the stretch of oak leaves as well as the pile of old ties. As mentioned earlier, most of the Groton Plantation was burned every year, leaving the ground black and charred. Such a background afforded little concealment. The small patch of unburned terrain might well have served as an island of protection for a snake so protectively colored.

On May 5, the ninth day of our watching, Canebrake came from his lair at ten in the morning and later lay with head pointing toward the woods. Somewhere between 1:30 and 4:00 PM he left us. I had supposed that, being nocturnal, he would have waited for night time.

When I say that Canebrake was handsome I refer to his body. A view of his head, seen at closest range with a pair of powerful binoculars, was a different matter. If one had to design a cover for a horror magazine, I doubt if one could think of anything more chilling to look at.

The scientific name of the Canebrake Rattlesnake is *Crotalus horridus*. The *horridus* applies to the head. The eyes, being mere slits by daylight, are what makes it so lifeless. The rest of the head is as angular and hard as if carved in stone and painted—a true death's head. Whenever I spent a minute or two looking at Canebrake's face, I thought, "this will come to me later in my dreams."

Actually it never has. The only other death's heads I have seen were those worn by Hitler's SS Troops during the war—men who struck down millions of their own kind without warning, without cause and in wanton cruelty. When I think of these things I think more kindly of my snakes, doubting whether any of them strikes unless feeling endangered. What they want is to be left alone, to enjoy the life to which they are so beautifully adapted. It is difficult to think of any predator that actually kills its prey more humanely than a rattlesnake. It can paralyze a small rodent in short fashion with one lightening stab.

As a naturalist, my heart warms to the idea that we should live and let live. It is we humans who can learn from nature how to live in a maximum of peace.

* * * * * * * * *

There were two other snake adventures at the plantation, one involving a very small snake and the other a large one. It was a miracle that I found the small one. I was wading into a swampy place to watch by a Red-headed Woodpecker's nest when I stopped to admire a green frog. I wanted to pause long enough to see him well. It was then that I saw a darkish worm move in the black mud. I made a quick swoop.

My prize was unbelievable. Entwining itself in my fingers was a half-grown ringneck snake five inches long, a beautiful bluish black snakelet with a golden collar just behind its head and a bright red belly with handsome black dots. It was an amazingly lucky find. Ring-necks are not overly difficult to find under stones, logs or bark near wet places, but they are almost never seen moving about in the open.

Had I not stopped to look at the frog as it sat surrounded by a thick growth of marsh grass and other plants, I never could have seen this tiny snake of the same color as the wet black mud from which the plants were growing. Truly, if one wants to find snakes, he has to learn to think snakes in all times and places. They can, at times, be exceedingly difficult to see.

Jane had the other adventure. While walking along a stretch of bare earth and low grass she noted a long thick snake stretched across the track ahead of her. The snake coiled back on itself in sudden alarm. Then it miraculously leaped clear of the ground as it swung its head backward to fall into the water of a marshy ditch, exposing the red of its belly as it did so. From Jane's description I gathered that she had seen a red-bellied water snake. I was most envious of her good fortune.

* * * * * * * * *

What conclusions can be drawn from our experiences? I had loved reptiles of all kinds as a boy and was taking pleasure in reverting to the interest in later years. Watching snakes would not have been the pleasure it was had it not been for the excellence of present-day bird glasses. Standing at the closest possible range of eight feet all objects, such as the pattern of a snake or its head, stood out larger and more clearly than if seen within inches.

It takes time to appreciate and study the marvel and beauty of most creatures, especially if they are partly concealed by vegetation. The person who grabs or tries to kill misses this. What I like is nature as undisturbed as possible. I did pick up snakes twice, but on the whole, I think the greatest dividends come from not interfering. This, at least, was a game I was trying to learn.

I am fond of quotations. Ideas encountered in reading, regardless of subject, give pleasure when one sees a relationship to one's own activities. It may seem remote from snakes, but a remark quoted in the age of Samuel Johnson was that the ideal for poets, writers, and scholars was to be men to whom "nothing human was alien." Certainly some thinkers of that enlightened age had broad sympathies with the human animal and much good came of it in the form of humanitarianism. Man became more kindly toward his fellow man.

A step beyond the humanist, I think, is the man who is both humanist and naturalist—the man to whom no living creature is alien. Such men have always been rare. At the beginning of the age of enlightenment there was one, Sir Thomas Browne and toward the end, another, Erasmus Darwin.

"I cannot start at the presence of a serpent, scorpion, lizard or salamander, at the sight of a toad or viper," wrote Browne. "I find in me no desire to take up a stone to destroy them." Erasmus Darwin extended his sympathies even to worms and insects.

The grand experience is to see nature as a harmony, as an undivided whole of which the snake, the insect, the bird is one with the watcher, to whom no creature is singled out as being alien. "All" wrote Emerson, "are needed by each one. Nothing is fair or good alone."

At Tuten's Plaza we felt these bonds with nature. But to tell the truth I was glad that Canebrake did not reciprocate to the extent of entering the shack. We liked him best, coiled where he was.

XII. DYING ELMS: BOON TO WOODPECKERS

"Nature often carries out experiments in front of one, and the only thing one has to do is to be on the alert, to appreciate the significance of what is seen and to cash in on the result."–N. Tinbergen.

Dutch Elm disease, however lamentable to man, has been a boon to woodpeckers. This was something I noted 20 years ago when I set out to learn what I could about woodpeckers.

Woodpeckers in general are not attracted to young, healthy woodlands. They prefer mature forests where large trees provide dead and dying limbs with tops broken by the wind. These harbor wood-boring larvae of beetles and other insects. Sometimes tree diseases provide similar situations.

If one can see good in tragedy, the benefactor of woodpeckers is the elm bark beetle, an invader from Europe only one-eighth of an inch in length that was harmless until it linked up with *Ceratocystis ulmi*. The team of beetle-plus-fungus created a disease that, in its wake, provided woodpeckers with populations of beetle larvae on which to feed. It also provided them with a supply of stubs for nesting—a supply that has lasted for many years.

Diseased elms are recognizable by the engraving of multi-branching tunnels made by the beetles for their eggs and larvae. While living in Maryland between 1956 and '61 I sometimes noted as many as four Downy Woodpeckers feeding on a single elm. Wherever the woodpeckers worked they chipped off outer layers, revealing the multiple tunnels against a background of fawn-colored inner bark.

When I moved to New Hampshire in 1961 I became particularly interested in studying the breeding, feeding and other habits of Hairy Woodpeckers. In an initial study from August through November, a remarkable fact emerged: 19 of 20 Hairies feeding on diseased elms were females. The woodpeckers did not visit the trees very much in December and January but did return to them in February. From then through April, when nesting began, I found females feeding on the elms on 31 and males on only two occasions.

These findings led me to study Hairies on a variety of trees. It was soon evident that they do, indeed, have sexual differences in feeding habits.

I noted repeatedly that females, moving from tree to tree to scale bark or to dig out superficial prey, were the more restless of the two. Males, in contrast, were more deliberate. They looked about, carefully selected a spot, then settled down to excavate larger prey lying deeper in dead and rotting wood. I might never have noted this difference had I not started my studies with dying elms.

Relative few observations had been made on sexual differences in the feeding habits of any avian species at that time. The best accounts were those on the extinct Huia of New Zealand. The female Huia had a long, curved bill suited to pulling beetle larvae from tunnels in old logs while her mate had a shorter, straight bill adapted to digging. Could Hairy Wood-

peckers also have bill differences? An unexpected result of publication of my findings was a statement by a
professional ornithologist. He had been measuring
bills of museum specimens and pointed out that there
is, on the average, a ten percent difference in bill
length between male and female Hairies.

One may ask why Hairies should have differences
in feeding habits. What may be the survival advantages in terms of natural selection? A usual explanation is that the birds of a pair are able to use the
resources of their habitat more effectively, one sex
not competing with the other in finding prey.

I believe that other factors may operate as well.
Hairy Woodpeckers have a long courtship beginning
in January. If they had similar feeding habits they
might interfere with one another. But with each
foraging in its own way they can be together without
competing. This, in turn, makes for a closer pair
bond.

* * * * * * * * * *

After elms have been dead for some years the
larger ones become attractive to Pileated Woodpeckers. If one happens to have such a stub in his back
yard he may have unusual opportunities for watching
these magnificent but seldom-seen birds.

Pileateds make huge bathtub-shaped excavations,
sometimes one to three feet high, four or more inches
wide and five to six inches deep. I found a Pileated
making an excavation early one morning in March.
The woodpecker was still at work in the same place
when I returned four hours later. The pile of chips
on the ground was considerable. While Pileated
Woodpeckers dig for the tunnels of carpenter ants in
hemlock and white pine, they are often after the

large, tunneling larvae of the pigeon horntail, among other prey, in dead elms.

Dead elms provide woodpeckers with nesting as well as feeding places. Species nesting in them include the Pileated, Hairy, Downy and Red-bellied Woodpeckers, the flicker and the Yellow-bellied Sapsucker. But if a stub stands in the open, the woodpeckers are likely to come to grief. Starlings, with devilish ingenuity, often wait until a pair of Hairies, flickers or Red-bellied Woodpeckers have completed a nest and then dispossess them with persistent attacks. The Starlings invariably win. Woodpeckers are more successful when they select stubs within woods because Starlings avoid holes that are partly concealed by leafy branches.

* * * * * * * * * *

If one is an amateur birder one needs all the hours he can get before or after work and on weekends to watch courtship, nesting and other activities in spring. One way to lose time is to follow a series of nests scattered miles apart.

The dead elms have come to my rescue in recent years. Three hundred yards from our house is a wooded swamp of three to four acres containing many dead and dying elms.

By concentrating on these in the spring of 1971 I found the nests of a pair of Downies, a pair of Hairies and one of flickers within close reach. Trails from one to the other enabled me to watch them all.

The following year Jane and I did even better, finding nests of Downy, Hairy, Yellow-bellied Sapsucker and of another hole-nester, the Red-breasted Nuthatch. This was not the end of our success for

Jane, exploring a lumber clearing not far away, found the nest of a Hairy.

When I unfolded the chair I use for bird watching in a thicket where I had a good view, I discovered that a pair of flickers were nesting in the same elm as the Hairies and a pair of sapsuckers in one close by. I was thus able to follow the comings and goings of three species while sitting in one place!

On another spring morning I found a pair of Downies and a pair of chickadees nesting in smaller elm stubs, making five nests in one clearing.

All of the 12 nests found in 1971 and '72 were successful, with one exception. Some predator broke open the nest of the Red-breasted Nuthatches. These energetic little birds promptly re-nested in another elm, using a hole vacated shortly before by a pair of Downies.

* * * * * * * * *

The pleasure Jane and I take in sitting and watching birds in a lumber clearing or wooded swamp in spring may seem tame to those who prefer to be in a group and on the go. But can nature be hurried?

Sitting for half an hour or so at a time we have seen many things in addition to the comings and goings of woodpeckers. There is enjoyment in merely watching the unfolding of ferns and flowers or, in the swamp, a Northern Waterthrush teetering like a small sandpiper as it deftly reaches into a dark pool to catch one mosquito larva after another.

These are the small and usual things. On rare occasions a deer has come close and once, while watching a flicker's nest, I heard a heavy crashing as a Black Bear came to a clearing 50 feet away. In these hours one comes to have a sense of interrelations of living things.

Spores of a fungus that have little means of traveling on their own adhere to a passing bark beetle that carries them under the bark of another elm. Here they proliferate, killing branches that give more places where the beetles can lay their eggs.

Elms die, woodpeckers come to feed and, years later, to nest. But they cannot nest in just any dead elm. It takes the concurrence of other kinds of fungi before the dead wood becomes sufficiently workable for even the strongest woodpecker to excavate a cavity.

After the woodpeckers have finished and the young have departed, the history of the hole has just begun. Red Squirrels often move into those left by Hairy Woodpeckers, finding a secure place to have and raise their young.

When I tap on such a tree in winter, a flying squirrel may peer out, his round head just fitting the entrance.

It is in winter that I go the rounds of my stubs to study the roosting habits of these woodpeckers and nuthatches continuing to use them.

The dying elms have now been a boon to woodpeckers and other creatures over many years. Unsightly as they are, they can also be of benefit to the naturalist who likes to find things to look for in all seasons and close to home.

XIII. BIRDS OF A HEMLOCK CONE YEAR

"Watching always brings the excitement of seeing something new. The feeding methods are especially fascinating because they are so immensely diverse."–N. Tinbergen.

No two winters are alike and this is a boon to the student of bird behavior. He need never run out of things to study.

For several winters I studied the feeding of Hairy Woodpeckers on dying elms; then for several more the feeding of Downies on coccids, small insects infesting the bark of paper birches. As usually happens when one starts watching, one makes discoveries and finds that we are far from knowing much about the behavior of some of our common birds.

Red-breasted Nuthatches were abundant during the fall of 1972. I decided to observe all I could about their activities. Doing so led me to note that hemlocks were bearing an unusually heavy crop of cones. What birds would come to this large supply of winter food? How long would it last?

Nearly all my observations were made within 100 yards of our cabin in the New Hampshire woods. Between mid-September and mid-October I noted that two Red-breasted Nuthatches, a male and a female, were storing seeds not of hemlocks but of balsams, in an area where they remained all winter. The male made flights to the top of a balsam, then flew to a maple about 10 yards away to poke a seed into a patch of lichen or crevice in bark.

I saw no flocking with chickadees at this time—in fact quite the reverse. Chickadees coming through the area were attacked by the nuthatches, once by displacing and once by pursuit in the air. But the main competitors for the balsam seeds, which were largely exhausted by mid-October, were red squirrels and Red Crossbills.

Hemlock cones mature in October and it was not until the 18th that I found nuthatches and chickadees feeding on them together. The two species differed in methods of storing. It might take 2-12 seconds for a nuthatch to extract seed from a cone, then 12-15 seconds to store it in some nearby hardwood. Sometimes the bird hid the seed in the rough bark of a hemlock.

Although associated as pairs in territories in the autumn, Red-breasted Nuthatches generally worked as separate individuals while storing and were, therefore, seldom close to one another.

A nuthatch commonly stored seeds by holding its head flat then poking the seed under a flake of bark. Hemlock seeds are so small that it was difficult for me to see just what was going on. The bird made quick jabs of its bill to the side, then poked back to the storage place. I saw clearly on several occasions that it was covering its stores with a fragment of bark.

The chickadees appeared less efficient, flying 12 to 20 yards to poke seeds into small crevices in outer twigs and small branches of various hardwoods. Their flights took a longer time. One would think from these contrasting methods that the nuthatches, by putting their stores in a smaller area, would have an easier time finding them later.

On the other hand the chickadees, with their wider dispersal of seeds, may have had a community type of storage: seeds stored by one individual being something that any one of the flock might find at a later date.

Although the Red-breasted Nuthatches moved with the chickadees from hemlock to hemlock, they were often the last to leave. On some occasions I noted that they flew to more distant storage places. This suggested that the chickadees (always outnumbering the nuthatches) may have exerted a competitive pressure that induced the latter to store in a restricted area they could watch and defend. But the storage methods of the two species were not invariable. The chickadees sometimes stored close to the hemlocks as well as at a distance.

I saw relatively little storing by either species in October. This may have been because both species found such an abundance of various foods including insects, that the hemlock seeds represented a surplus not needed for immediate consumption. Storing did not begin in earnest until November.

* * * * * * * * *

Chickadees, clinging to cones upside down, appeared to be more efficient than the nuthatches at extracting seeds. The Red-breasted Nuthatches, in contrast, resorted to a number of methods. They might perch next to a cone to poke with their longer bills; cling to a cone; or occasionally flutter below, then fly to some small crevice or anvil to knock the two vanes from the winged seed. One could sometimes see the small vanes floating downward.

Neither species was adept as the Pine Siskins. These birds crowded in numbers of 50 or more on one hemlock, extracting and consuming seeds all in one operation. A seeming result of this efficiency was that they had an ample margin of leisure. I often saw them preening and resting in the sun. Not so with the chickadees. They kept moving from morn until dark as though needing all the time they had to feed.

Although always busy when with chickadees, the nuthatches often rested when alone, hanging upside down against a tree trunk. When one of the pair was resting, I would nearly always find its mate resting also.

* * * * * * * * * *

Effects of Weather. The cones of hemlock trees, being hydroscopic, are strikingly affected by weather. They open on dry, cold and windy days and close, as one might expect, on warmer more humid ones. The winter of 1972-73 was unusually warm. On days and weeks of mild weather, the scales of the cones closed and chickadees visited hemlocks infrequently. I found nuthatches difficult to locate at such times and seldom saw them.

A light snowfall on November 5 covered all twigs and branches. I saw no birds until I came to a grove of hemlocks whose flat branches had kept the ground free of snow. Here were 20 or more chickadees, possibly two flocks combined; a pair of Red-breasted and one of White-breasted Nuthatches, and a number of Golden-crowned Kinglets.

These species were rarely associated with flocks of chickadees when the latter fed on hemlocks on other days. It seemed, therefore, that the snow had had the effect of bringing them together.

Chickadees and Red-breasted Nuthatches foraged on hemlock seeds that had fallen to the ground. This type of foraging became more pronounced as the season progressed—especially after snow had lain on the ground for some days and seeds, shaken from cones by wind or other agencies, had time to accumulate.

On three occasions I saw Pine Grosbeaks feeding alongside the smaller birds. Their thick bills were covered on the outside with the small, severed vanes of hemlock seeds.

It seemed unlikely that these larger birds could have fed on the small hemlock cones directly and I did not see them doing so. The snow crust afforded their only opportunity to feed on the seeds. Pine Grosbeaks keep to themselves when feeding high in pines and maples and it was only when down on the snow that I saw them associating.

The weeks of desultory feeding on hemlocks in November and December ended, almost dramatically, with the onset of temperatures near -20°C in the second week of January. Scales of cones opened to their full extent in the drier air associated with lower temperatures, wind and sun. The chickadees and Red-breasted Nuthatches were once more associated, sometimes concentrating on just a few hemlocks where I was able to watch them for hours at a time.

While the chickadees and nuthatches foraged mainly on the cones, they also spent considerable time on the snow below, picking up seeds shaken loose by the wind. Both species generally went to the snow at the same time, as though one species was affected by the movements of the other. I no longer saw large flocks of siskins. By this time they were mostly in small numbers of three or four that were frequently associated with the chickadees.

These optimal conditions ended in less than a week. With a return of milder weather, associations of Red-breasted Nuthatches and chickadees became infrequent.

There was a return of intensely cold weather on February 1 and again on February 11. It now seemed that the supply of hemlock seeds had become exhausted during the January cold spell. The hemlocks were no longer visited by birds of any species.

As for the total crop of hemlock seeds, the chickadees and nuthatches had probably taken only a small part. Red Squirrels were abundant and had continued to feed on cones regardless of weather in the late fall and early winter. It was likely that they and the large flocks of siskins had been the heaviest users of this unusually large crop of seeds, many of which were dispersed by the wind.

* * * * * * * * * *

Reaction to a Shrike. One might expect that aggregations of birds in one place would attract some predator. Until I began watching flocks of small winter birds, my thinking had been largely in terms of hawks. But there is another predator in winter months.

I was watching a flock of about eight chickadees on January 8 when they all disappeared with great suddenness. I then caught a glimpse of a Northern Shrike. The shrike moved through the centers of two

hemlocks where the chickadees had been feeding, before flying off. A few minutes later the hemlocks,
almost miraculously, became alive with chickadees
again.

* * * * * * * * *

A question is why the Red-breasted Nuthatches
should have flocked with chickadees on days when
the hemlock cones were open and not on other days?
As hemlock trees were everywhere, why could they
not have fed just as well by themselves?

One might guess that the association gave better
protection against predators. Although this is a common argument, I am not sure. Flocks are what seem
to attract predators and so are something of a hazard.
Furthermore, avian predators in New Hampshire, of
a size likely to attack small birds, are rare in winter
woods in daylight.

My feeling is that the association of nuthatches and
chickadees was for other reasons.

The bumper crop of hemlock seeds was expend-
able and due to last for a few months only. The largest
depleters of the crop were the red squirrels, the Pine
Siskins that came by hundreds, and the winter winds.

Faced with this competition, how could the nuthatches and chickadees get the most of the crop on the limited number of days when cones were open?

I think the flocking was important in inducing social facilitation. The nuthatches, surrounded by also-foraging chickadees, were driven to work harder themselves—harder than if they had been alone. This meant that they took in more seed and more of the energy available.

In these terms the flocking of Red-breasted Nuthatches and chickadees in a hemlock cone year may have had value in survival and been a product of natural selection.

It is not enough just to look at birds if one wants to get full enjoyment. It is both watching and wondering that makes the study of bird behavior rewarding. One needs to ask the question "What is the importance of this or that activity to survival?" One may not find the right answer, but the search will lead one back to the woods to make more observations.

This at least is one of the pleasures I have found . . . even in the depths of winter in New Hampshire.

XIV. A NATURAL HISTORY OF SAPSUCKERS

"Natural history is one of the few sciences–that may also claim a place among the humanities. It demands of its students not only close observation and exact knowledge but imaginative gifts far more commonly associated with, for example, the study of literature. It is a realm of pure beauty."–W. A. Breyfogle.

There are attractions to studying Yellow-bellied Sapsuckers in a New Hampshire summer.

If one is not in a hurry and will take the time to watch a male until it catches the light, one will see what a beautiful bird he is: black and white markings, a brilliant red throat and crown and yellow below the black bib of his chest. As an amateur I do not hesitate to put the beauty of a bird first.

Another attraction to sapsuckers is that one can go to woods in July or August and find them returning to the same trees day after day. I have spent hours watching them taking sap at their bands of drill holes; a male, female and three or four juveniles forming a family group. Sometimes I have perched in an adjacent tree ten feet away, so close that field glasses were not needed.

Few birds provide food for such a variety of other creatures. Among these are Black-throated Blue and

Cape May Warblers along with butterflies, black hornets, chipmunks and red squirrels. The list is actually much longer.

The most steady customer is the Ruby-throated Hummingbird. In looking for sapsucker trees where the woods were new to me, I have often located them by the hum of a hummingbird. Hummers start following sapsuckers as soon as they arrive in May and continue to do so well into September. So closely are they attracted that they sometimes follow sapsuckers to their nest holes.

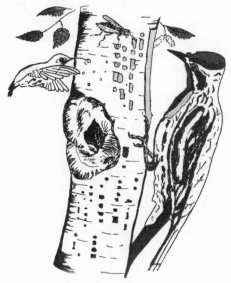

As leaves change color and begin to fall in September, first adult then juvenile sapsuckers begin to disappear. But like Hermit Thrushes and Winter Wrens they are hardy and will be among the first to return in April when woods are still patchy with snow.

* * * * * * * * *

A fortunate aspect of my woodpecker studies was that they began when we were living in Maryland and only spending summers in New Hampshire. I thus had a chance not only to watch Red-bellied and other southern woodpeckers, but also sapsuckers on their winter range.

Sapsuckers, with the mottled browns, white, and blacks of their backs blending in with the bark to which they clung, were difficult to locate on most winter days. It was only on warmer days, when sap flowed, that they became excited, visiting holes from the bottoms to the tops of trees and making "waan" notes as they did so.

White-breasted Nuthatches, Tufted Titmice, Carolina Chickadees and others joined in taking sap. Owning sapsuckers tried to drive these intruders away, but usually with little success.

Red-bellied Woodpeckers also came for sap. On one occasion, when a sapsucker tried to drive a Red-bellied away, I saw the larger bird seize the sapsucker by the nape of the neck and hold it dangling in its bill for a moment before letting it go . . . one of the odder sights I have seen in years of bird watching.

A curious feature of distribution is that male sapsuckers winter farther north than females, the latter being found as far south as Florida and the West Indies. A few years ago I encountered a sapsucker a short distance from the Panama Canal; my farthest south to date. I have also studied sapsuckers in the Gaspé Peninsula in Canada. No other North American woodpecker has such an extended range in migration. Sapsuckers are, indeed, one of the most migratory of woodpeckers.

* * * * * * * * * *

There is no more delightful season in Vermont and New Hampshire than early April when freezing nights and thawing days make the sap flow. At this time, when snow still lies in the woods, male sapsuckers arrive a week or so before their mates.

Man has to boil the winter sap stored in trunks of sugar maples to concentrate it, for it is too watery to have flavor. Sapsuckers, drinking lots of it, do the concentrating in their kidneys, as one can see by the amounts of silvery excreta they keep shooting outward.

Summer sap, elaborated in leaves and coming down through sapwood, is more concentrated. Flow in thin sheets from sapsucker holes and exposure to breezes and warm air concentrate it even further. One has only to lick the bands of holes to find this out for himself.

Sapsuckers do not take sap merely for a drink. Sap that can carry enough nutrients to build a huge sugar maple can be nutritious for sapsuckers, hummingbirds and other creatures as well.

* * * * * * * * * *

If one is accustomed to getting up early in the morning there is no more startling sound in April woods than the drumming of a male sapsucker against a resonating place. (I will not specify a dead tree because sapsuckers like whatever place makes the most noise; whether it be a tin gutter, a fence post, or a telephone line.) The drumming, a "dr-rr-aa-da-da-da", comes in unusually long bursts . . . so loud and staccato that I am reminded of a Bofors, an anti-aircraft gun used in World War II.

When Jane and I were entering Baxter State Park in Maine one June, the guard said a sapsucker woke him every morning at 4:30 drumming on the front fender of his car. As we stood watching, the bird came and performed for us, just three feet off the ground.

If one continues to watch sapsuckers in April woods, one may see colorful performances. I call these dances, because they are a patterned and rhythmic succession of movements. Two males face each other four to five inches apart, jerking their bodies straight up and down as they make scratchy "quirk" notes. With necks elongated, displaying the red of their throats, and with red crests raised like cockades, the spectacle appears almost military.

After a few moments one or the other may fly low and away displaying the black and white pattern of his back to the accompaniment of a loud winnow noise.

What is the meaning of these displays?

All are means of communicating, the message depending on the context of attendant circumstances.

My interpretations differ from those of some, who lump such displays together as being aggressive. Being aggressive means a desire to inflict injury. I have seen no sign of this in the dances of sapsuckers, flickers or other woodpeckers. Rather, the dances are an effort to persuade by peaceful means.

One male persuades another to move on, to space out in relation to territory. When two males want to fight—as they may later in the breeding season after the females have arrived—there are no displays. With plumage sleeked down the two go at each other in silence, usually low to the ground. One may grapple with the other as small feathers are seized and pulled. But such physical clashes are rare. It is more common for one sapsucker to fly at, then pursue another in swift flight through the woods.

* * * * * * * * * *

Woodpeckers are unlike passerine birds such as the Song Sparrow, where the female is the dominant partner. She selects the nest site, builds the nest, then lays and incubates the eggs. The situation is different among woodpeckers. Here, while the female shares the duties of excavating, incubating, and feeding the young, it is the male that is the more domestic.

Although the pair bonds of woodpeckers are close, there are occasions for disagreements. A male sapsucker may choose a dead stub and start to excavate. He would like to carry on but he needs the approval of his mate. This he seeks by giving loud "queeark" breeding calls. He is on the lookout and as soon as he sees his mate coming, he starts tapping with his bill against the rim of his excavation.

Tapping is not miscellaneous pecking in search of food nor is it fast, like drumming. It is a slow, evenly

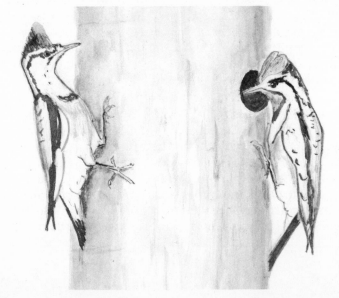

spaced tap-tap-tap used by woodpeckers of many species in an effort of one partner to secure the approval of the other as to a choice of nest site. When a female sapsucker alights close to her mate, who is tapping, she does a bobbing dance indicating her excitement. The male then flies away in a winnow flight. Or the situation may occur in reverse when she, being at the hole, taps while he alights and dances.

It is one thing to describe these performances but quite anther to watch them in late April or early May when the shad bush and other spring flowers are emerging, Hermit Thrushes singing and Ruffed Grouse drumming.

* * * * * * * * * *

Members of a pair of sapsuckers may spend weeks trying to agree on a nest site. The female is more cautious and conservative and so she may cease to join with the male in tapping or dancing if a stub appears too rotten or unsafe. The search for another site leads to more drumming, breeding calls and winnow flights.

Once the members of a pair have agreed on a site they cease their displays and become increasingly quiet. During these silent periods the female rests motionless or preens in a leisurely fashion while her mate does the larger share of the excavating. Colorful displays are no longer needed as the time of mating approaches.

Ralph Waldo Emerson wrote that "The length of the discourse indicates the distance of thought between the speaker and the hearer. If they were at perfect understanding—no words would be necessary thereon. If at one in all parts, no words would be suffered."

The discourse of woodpeckers is by drumming, tapping and displays. But otherwise is not the phenomenon the same? Silence reflects understanding.

* * * * * * * *

The time of egg-laying, incubation and of feeding the young can proceed so uneventfully as to be something of an anticlimax to the intense activities of earlier weeks. The sapsuckers form an efficient team in all they do. Their comings and goings to brood or to feed are swift and silent except when exchanging "yerk, yerk" notes by way of recognition when they happen to meet.

Nestlings begin making steady harsh noises as soon as they hatch. These increase in volume as they grow older. They become so loud that one can use them to locate a sapsucker's nest, even from 100 yard away.

What is the function of this clamor? Could it not be harmful in attracting predators such as raccoons, weasels, hawks or owls?

Here one should recall that natural selection is always a compromise. There must be survival advantages to such a volume of sound that outweigh the disadvantages.

My guess is that the noise of the young is not so uniform as it first sounds but fluctuates in volume, pitch and in quality of harshness to softness at the time of being fed. It is a broadcast of conditions at the nest that parents can hear even when foraging at a distance.

The chief message is one of "hurry, hurry, hurry"—or so I think when I see parents coming with food every three minutes. They almost never seem to stop. It is difficult to see how they can work any harder.

What do parents feed their young? Sapsuckers, quick on the wing and agile in hitching up tree trunks, are expert flycatchers. Their bills are stuffed with insects within a few minutes of leaving the nest.

One might think this load of prey enough but sapsuckers have a double food supply. Each parent, before returning to the nest with insects, usually stops by a band of drill-holes to take sap as well. The load of insects does not interfere.

Sapsuckers flying to nests enter without delay. Then, after a minute, they may emerge slowly and gingerly with a large load of fecal matter mixed with sawdust and fly to some tree trunk to shake it loose.

The nestlings are ready to leave after four weeks—a long time to be in a nest compared with open-nesters such as Robins and Song Sparrows. A fledgling may occupy the entrance, sticking its head way out then pulling it back. Sometimes it strikes down at a parent coming to feed it.

Then the exciting moment comes. The nestling leans out too far, loses control, and flies off on its first flight. This may end on a tree trunk or, with less skill, on the ground. What is surprising is how well a fledgling is able to manage itself. Although unable to catch insects, fledglings can take sap from holes drilled by parents. They are thus, in some degree, able to feed themselves from the very start.

* * * * * * * * * *

Having followed sapsuckers through to fledging, we should stop to consider that not all pairs are suc-

cessful. Some fail to nest. Others lose nests to predators and other causes determined by an intertwining
of ecologic factors. To understand these one needs an
interest in forestry and the habitat in general.

When I first studied sapsuckers it was not difficult
to find nesting pairs in any direction I might walk
from our house in Tamworth, New Hampshire. The
activities of each pair excited neighboring pairs and
the woods resounded with drumming in early May.
Why this population abundance? I think, in retrospect, that it was due to the hurricanes and lumbering
that went on during and after World War II.

Lumbered areas contained broken stubs ideal for
woodpeckers. I keep wishing today that I could find
the nests of Hairy and Downy Woodpeckers and
Yellow-bellied Sapsuckers as readily as I did then.
Trees or stubs suitable for the nesting of any of these
birds are generally in short supply; their scarcity
being a factor limiting woodpeckers.

If woodpeckers could carve their nest holes in any
healthy tree one of their main problems would be
solved. We would probably see more of them than we
do. The provision of decaying stubs as a result of
lumbering was something of a bonanza.

The supply of these was largely exhausted by the
late 1950's. In 1958 I watched a pair of sapsuckers
nesting in a dead maple. They tried to use it again the
following year but, unable to find a place suitable for
excavating, they investigated a number of other sites.
Each time there was dancing, tapping and winnow
flights; all to no avail. Their territory contained no
place to nest. The two sapsuckers spent the remainder of the breeding season flying around their territorial borders, picking fights with their neighbors.

When we moved to Lyme in the early 1960's I found sapsuckers more plentiful than today. They were nesting in two types of habitat. One was the lumbered areas suffering from post-logging decadence and the other, surprisingly, in woods never lumbered. These latter, containing many aspens, were ones that had sprouted in farm fields 60 to 70 years previously.

As the aspens matured they became weakened by competition with stronger growing, longer-lived forest trees such as maples and birches. Some developed conspicuous conks of the tinder fungus *Fomes igniarius*. These, I came to find, are the main nest trees of sapsuckers. I have learned to look for them when hunting for sapsucker nests. Of 65 nests found in New Hampshire, 43 were in *Fomes*-aspens. Why should this be?

A theory borne out by experience is that *Fomes*-aspens are ideal nest trees. The sapsuckers usually excavate nest entrances a foot or so above or below a conk. The first inch or two of tough sapwood makes hard going. But once sapsuckers reach the soft heartwood decayed by the fungus it is easy for them to excavate a large, deep cavity.

The situation is ideal; first in providing a cavity surrounded by tough, living wood that can keep out predators; and second, by the fact that a good *Fomes*-aspen can be used for renesting in succeeding years. I followed one aspen in which sapsuckers nested for six years, building a fresh cavity each year. This situation is unusual among woodpeckers. Species such as Hairies, Downies and Pileateds never re-nest in any one tree, at least in my experience.

* * * * * * * * * *

There are signs that one can associate with raccoon attacks on a nest. One is the presence of wisps of hair caught on rough bark and another, wing and tail feathers piled on the ground below where an adult male or a well grown young one has been devoured. A third and striking sign is a rosette of tooth marks around the hole, made when a raccoon has gnawed hard, but has been unable to get through the outer shell of sapwood.

One nest, destroyed in 1967, was only six feet above the ground—the lowest nest I have found. A rosette of marks appeared early in the nesting season with no effect on the parents who continued to feed their young. Then other tooth marks appeared as the raccoon attacked on successive nights.

The entrance came to look like a battlefield. The racoon finally succeeded in catching the adult male as well as the young—possibly by dangling a long leg and paw inside.

The predator might have been less persistent had the sapsuckers excavated their hole higher up. But as in all aspens, sapsuckers have to carve their holes where conks are located. If there are no locations higher up, they may be forced to nest low to the ground or not at all.

* * * * * * * * * *

Having discussed the depredations of one predator, we might pause to consider evolution and natural selection. This is an approach that Julian Huxley says "will prompt us to ask the right questions of nature, and, when we have asked them, will help us to find the right answers."

Predation is one of the strongest of selection pressures. Sapsuckers that developed a search image of a

secure nest site survived to raise their young despite
the loss of a few. The genes of those nesting in weak,
rotting stubs that might be torn or chewed open by
predators, on the contrary, were often eliminated
from the gene pool. By such a process, each kind of
woodpecker developed a search image of the optimal
nest site for its species—the one offering the most
protection.

To advance a theory such as this is to invite attack,
especially if one publishes in a professional journal.
This is good, in a way. What is better for one's ideas
than the pruning effect of criticism? But criticism
should be sound to be effective.

Two biologists studying sapsuckers found them
nesting in aspens with no raccoons in attendance. *Ipso
facto*, according to these biologists, my ideas on the
search image of nest sites did not hold in the main
part of the sapsucker's range. But does not this express biological *naiveté*?

Neither sapsuckers nor man evolved under conditions which exist today. Evolution is a process taking
place over hundreds of thousands of years. To recon-
struct sapsucker evolution, one should imagine conditions as they were in pre-Columbian times; a conti-
nent of virgin forest inhabited by predators whose
populations had never been decimated by steel traps
or other means. Raccoons may have never existed
over much of the sapsuckers' range, but their place as
tree climbing predators would have been taken by
weasels, martin, fishers and others.

How can one imagine that the evolution of nesting
habits in sapsuckers took place without predation,
when it is one of the strongest of selection pressures?

* * * * * * * * * *

Some aspens became so riddled with nest holes in successive years that I called them apartment nest trees. I have amused myself in fall and winter months making rounds to see who might be living in them.

If I knocked on the trunks enough times, over a number of months, I almost invariably saw a flying squirrel. Sometimes I found a hole well-gnawed and enlarged. When I knocked below such a hole, the heads of three and even four flying squirrels might pop out at a time.

I think flying squirrels enlarge holes so that all can escape simultaneously, if need be. While red and even grey squirrels also occupy old nest cavities, flying squirrels appear to be the chief beneficiaries of those made by sapsuckers.

* * * * * * * * * *

Interrelations of living things are endless. Sapsuckers returning to carve a nest in spring tolerate flying squirrels that have moved in the fall or winter before. On a number of occasions I have found the two species, bird and mammal, living in holes only two to three feet apart.

Both Jane and I have seen the odd sight of a female sapsucker hitching up gingerly to have a look at a

flying squirrel neighbor. The reaction of the squirrel was to swing completely out, then quickly back into its hole. This served to drive the sapsucker away but never from the tree itself. The two species, it seems, are adjusted to being neighbors.

From winter activities to the arrival in spring, to courtship, nesting and summers spent in family groups, I have had much pleasure in watching the colorful lives of sapsuckers. There is so much to learn. In another 20 years, perhaps, I can come up with more complete answers.

In the meantime I think of the words of Gilbert White. "My remarks" he wrote, "are the result of many years observation; and are I trust true in the whole, though I do not pretend to say that they are perfectly void of mistakes, or that a more nice observer might not make many additions, since subjects of this kind are inexhaustible."

XV. BEHAVIOR OF TWO YOUNG CROWS

"Who are the people with whom the higher animals are most serene, and who achieve most success in their management and training? Not those who look upon them as automata, but those who treat them as likeable children of our own kind."—F. Fraser Darling.

Joe, our first crow, was a blue-eyed youngster about to leave his nest when a neighborhood newsboy brought him to us.

He merely sat on our front porch, squatting close and refusing to eat for the first few days. We thought him a rather hopeless pet. It seemed likely that he had come to us a little too old to be tamed. We had to pry open his bill to feed him, pushing bread and milk down his cavernous gullet with slightly nervous fingers. I then had an idea.

I had read of a young oriole that fed readily from an orange-colored dropper, but not from droppers of other colors. Black might have a similar effect upon Joe. Accordingly we shaped a crow's bill from wooden forceps and stained it with India ink. Jane covered her hand with a black cloth and made flapping motions like a parent bird coming to the nest. Joe responded by opening his mouth and begging— something he had not done before.

The artificial bill made feeding easier for the next few days, but Joe remained suspicious of us. When sufficiently developed he made for a tree and, with combined hops and flops, worked his way up. By noontime he was cawing for food in the treetop with no idea of how to come down. He continued to caw miserably all afternoon and evening. The neighbor boy finally climbed up and fetched him. Joe's attitude had softened somewhat as a result of his difficulties. He now took all the food we offered, his clamoring cries halting only when gulping down large morsels.

When I stepped onto the back porch the following morning, Joe cawed from the roof in anticipation. With a few awkward swerves he came down for breakfast. At last, I thought, we are getting acquainted.

Just as the relationship showed signs of improving, Joe disappeared. I called "Here, Joe, here, Joe!", but no response came at the breakfast hour. As the day passed Jane and I felt that Joe had flown off to join his own kind. We were resigned to our loss. Then half a week later a neighbor remarked that soot had been falling into his fireplace. Investigation showed that Joe was perched above the grate. I imagined that he would be ragged and emaciated after 3½ days without food or water. But such was not the case. He appeared bright and well-preserved. The darkness of his prison may have had an hypnotic effect; preventing useless struggles and exhaustion.

Joe's delight in seeing us was pathetic. He nestled close in Jane's lap, made contented noises and ate a prodigious amount. From that time on he trusted us completely. No animal could have shown humans more attention or affection than Joe gave to our entire family.

The lad who had given Joe to us had kept a litter mate in a cage. The bird clamored so loudly in early-morning hours that the boy's parents said it must go. It was thus that we acquired our second crow.

We welcomed her and so did Joe (though the feminine gender was applied only to simplify relationships; we never learned whether she was Joe's brother or sister). The birds were nearly identical and we called either one Joe. Their bills were slender and their usual notes soft and gull-like.

We thought they might be Fish Crows, for they had come from a golf course where such birds nested. A young Common Crow, to which I compared them, had a heavier bill. But as our birds grew older, their caws sounded increasingly like those of Common Crows. We never really learned which species they were. Possibly in an impressionable state, they had learned their regular caw notes from Common Crows passing over the yard.

Both crows loved companionship. If there was no one outside, the birds flew around the house looking in windows. If the baby was on the lookout, the crows alighted on the sill by his crib.

They were always alert to the opening of an outside door. When I went out to work, one alighted on my left shoulder, the other on my right. They ran their bills through my hair, pulled grass that I clenched between my teeth, or played with sticks I wiggled on the lawn. Sometimes when I sat on the porch, their sharp bills made concentrated attacks on my shoe-strings. One might then jump to my arm, loosening my wrist-watch, leaving the other to attack my belt buckle. Buttons aroused interest, particularly if loose. Anything a bit weak and easily torn—such as a minor rip in old clothing—was their delight.

The garden pool was another source of amusement. They ducked under the surface and splashed with gusto. Their feathers shed water poorly. They became so sodden in hard rains that patches of white skin showed through and they could hardly fly. Yet however miserable, the crows always refused to come indoors.

When tired of playing, one crow might go by himself to roost in a pine tree and carry on a soliloquy of croaks and caws not unlike human conversation. When the baby was brought out to his playpen, the crows swooped down from the treetops. The baby spoke their language. Both crows, perching on the rail of the pen, made guttural noises in response to the babblings of the infant.

All three liked the same playthings, such as bottle tops and a small silver bell on a string. Joe Crow watched Joshua Kilham playing with bell and string until Joshua's attention was diverted. Then one Joe or the other seized it quick as a flash and it was Joshua's turn to try to get it back. The crows were able to strike sharp blows, but they never hurt the baby—in spite of Joshua's impetuous grabbings of a wing or tail.

Our pets had a "ca-a-a" alarm note given at the approach of a dog or other danger. One morning there seemed to be no inciting cause, yet the crows were unusually excited and refused to eat. I finally spotted a black snake, another of our adopted friends, gliding slowly through a crack in the top of his cage below the porch.

* * * * * * * * * *

A friend had warned us that he once had a pet crow to which he was considerably attached, although it had cost him the good will of his neighbors. His crow

liked, among other things, to pull up seedlings and pick flowers; to follow the milkman on his rounds, removing bottle-tops, and to take letters from mail-boxes.

Our crows behaved well in comparison. They found sufficient entertainment and diversion with the children and the pool. But there was little doubt of their destructive talents. Even a stoutly-bound medical journal would disintegrate beneath a series of well-directed blows. Yet the crows did no serious damage and were good about not waking us too early in the morning, as pet crows are apt to do.

I did not learn until later that they followed the paper boy, thus accounting for their early-morning quiet. Their game was to unroll newspapers before tearing up the front page. If neighbors complained, I heard nothing of it.

One day two bare-legged boys came into the yard. They were strangers, and the crows greeted them by pecking at their legs. When the boys started to run, the crows were delighted. Hovering over their heads, the two Joes drove the boys screaming from the yard. Such incidents indicated that the crows had a close attachment to our family but not to outsiders.

* * * * * * * * *

Trouble developed when Jane and the children went to our place in New Hampshire, leaving me

alone for a time in Bethesda. The crows felt the loss
of companionship immediately. I had to go to work
everyday and was not too much help. Like neglected
children the two Joes rapidly became delinquents.
They took to tearing up flower beds in adjacent yards
in a matter of days. Unhappy rumors began to circu-
late about our "buzzards" (as one lady called them).
Each day new horror stories spread along the
grapevine, the worst being that the crows attacked
and frightened small children. I even caught them
tearing at the upholstery on a neighbor's somewhat
ancient car.

Yet the crows were so affectionate that I could not
face the prospect of losing them. They welcomed me
when I returned from work, alighting on my shoulders and pulling at my shoe laces in their old familiar
manner. How could I possibly part with them?

Neighborhood pressure soon indicated that I had
little choice.

It was a sad evening when I put the two crows into
the car and drove ten miles into the country. I freed
them by an old pasture gate, on a lonely dirt road.
Only one flew into a tree. Joe, our original bird,
sensed that not all was right and clung to me plead-
ingly.

How could I push him away? I put him on the front
of the car, thinking that—as I started to drive—he

would flop off as he did at home. He placed himself, instead, in front of the windshield and clung there in desperation. I got out of the car, tossed him into the air, then drove off. How wretched I felt, abandoning babes in the wood.

I did not want to desert my friends, but the alternative seemed to be police action and law suits.

The next morning, nonetheless, I found myself driving to the country and up the same lonely road. I stopped by the pasture gate. Not a crow was in sight. Crawling under the bars, I walked to the middle of the field.

"Here, Joe," I called hopelessly, "Here, Joe, here, Joe."

Then from far away across the valley I heard a familiar "caw, caw." Straight toward me came a crow, as fast as it could fly. It circled down, landing on my shoulder and rubbing its bill affectionately in my hair.

"Here, Joe, here, Joe," I called again and from another direction, deep in the woods, came an answering "caw". Out came the second crow, flapping down to settle on my other shoulder.

We got into the car, both crows clinging to me. Their joy at returning home was obvious to see. We played our old games that afternoon, forgetting that fate hung over us.

A police car drove to our gate the next morning. The officer asked if I had pet crows. "Yes," I replied, wondering what had happened this time. A man three streets away had applied for permission to shoot crows because some had drilled a hole in the

roof of his sedan. The man fortunately thought they were wild crows, not knowing of our pets.

* * * * * * * * * *

I heard of a fellow in the country who liked pets and I brought the crows to him. There, in a small village, the neighbors took kindly to the young crows—in fact envying their new owner. One crow unwrapped some loaves of bread on the porch of the general store, but the store owner had a welcome for the crows whenever they came for more.

It was a year before Jane and I dared stop.

Only one crow, our second one, was nearby. He did not seem to recognize us. He (or she) was the only crow anyone could feed by hand. Our original Joe never came close to anyone after leaving us. He stayed in the vicinity, apparently, because of close association with his sibling. Neither one took interest in the wild crows that occasionally came around.

Thus our original Joe, whose affection we had won with such effort, remained wild and suspicious of other people. His ordeal in the darkened chimney without food or water for three days had, it seemed, attached him with deep affection to us alone. We, on our part, felt that our crows had been likeable children of our own kind. The bond between us had been strong and it had tugged at our heart strings to let them go.

XVI. OWLS IN THE LIBRARY AND IN THE YARD

"I rejoice that there are owls. They represent the stark, twilight unsatisfied thoughts I have. Let owls do the idiotic and maniacal hooting for men. This sound suggests the infinite roominess of nature, that there is a world in which owls live."–H. D. Thoreau.

That two adult Great Horned Owls came to live with us for a time was nothing I had planned. They were given to us.

I placed them in my library thinking that, as birds of wisdom, they would look best against a background of books. I have never cared much for mounted birds. The owls, however, looked like stuffed ones when perched upright and motionless on their log above a bookcase. This was until one noted their eyes. These were their most expressive feature. The yellow irises enlarged or contracted the dark pupils with each turn of the head or varying emotion. Sometimes one eye winked followed by the other. The nictating membrane slid across at times in a second kind of winking. All these movements, accompanied by raisings and lowerings of short facial feathers, made the owls very expressive in ways of their own.

One day a couple strange to us drove to our gate. The lady jumped out and rushed to the door. Could she use our telephone? With no time for explanations I simply pointed to the library. After a few minutes I heard a shriek. The lady, although in great haste when she came in, left the house even faster, flinging herself hysterically on her husband's shoulder. I do not know what she said but I could imagine the effect of her suddenly perceiving two stuffed owls winking down at her as she grabbed the phone. Had she entered a mad house?

The owls usually sat where they were placed but were always alert to what was going on. This was especially so when I came each evening with a supply of dead laboratory mice. Bo, our first acquired owl, liked to be fed by hand. The feeding was a weird experience for Bo, holding the head of a mouse in his beak, he would gaze at the ceiling with a fixed stare as though something momentous was about to happen. There was no winking. A look almost of terror slowly developed as Bo closed his eyes, tossed his head back, and swallowed the mouse whole. After a few convulsive gulps and snaps of his bill, he was ready for more. Six or eight mice usually sufficed.

But the swallowing was not always complete with one gulp. Sometimes a mouse's tail remained curled around one of Bo's eyes. At such times a bib of white feathers bulged over the wad of mice already swallowed but still resting above the sternal notch.

Great Horned Owls have a heavy type of saliva not unlike the slime left by a snail's trail. This helps such prey as mice to slide down. It also coats the pellets which come back up within the next 20 hours, for owls regurgitate bones, fur and other indigestibles.

If Bo picked up a mouse and dropped it, our pet skunk would not touch it, presumably finding the saliva distasteful. Great Horned Owls naturally prey on skunks. Bo, however, showed little interest in our skunk even when the two shared the same armchair

of an evening. Both liked to be stroked if Jane or I sat in the chair with them. Bo was obstreperous when first picked up, but would settle down and almost purr with continued petting. The owls often suggested cats in postures and expressions.

Our pets occasionally shed fluffy feathers, each of which had the peculiar ability, possibly electrostatic, of clinging wherever it fell. It was difficult to shake one from a finger or to pick one up from a carpet. This was one of the less desirable features of Great Horned Owls as pets in relation to housekeeping.

When Bo got mad, which he frequently did in his earliest days with us, he would hiss and clap his bill like a castanet. His feet were so powerful that he could make bones in my hand numb with pain, even under a heavy glove.

The claws of a Great Horned Owl are unique compared to those of other common owls. When the toes are spread, the claws twist sideways in opposite directions. Driven into the back of some victim such as a skunk, these ¾-inch talons would be solidly locked by the criss-crossing. A leather glove, fortunately for me, was the most I ever had to pry loose. I was usually able to handle both owls with bare hands.

Virginia was our other bird. The boy who gave her to us kept falcons and she came equipped with jesses. She was beautiful and alert. As with our crows—we did not really know whether Bo was a male or Virginia a female. The genders seemed to fit, because Bo was thickset and powerful and Virginia more slender.

Virginia was surprisingly gentle. When I picked her up by having her climb onto my wrist, she used her claws no more than did our pet crow. She ate with less effort than Bo. If I held up a live mouse I would deftly take it from my fingers, scrunch and swallow it in a jiffy. Sometimes she would hold the mouse in one claw, or if her appetite had been appeased, tuck it by the log.

Bo and Virginia got on well together except when Virginia, getting on the perching log first, sat in Bo's corner. Bo would not rest or eat until, by making so much noise sparring with her, I was forced to put Virginia back in her proper place. The two owls frequently exchanged chuckling notes as if having owly conversations.

In spite of their docility and the full dinner-pail I sensed that both felt the call of the wild. There were, moreover, additional reasons for freeing them. Our house was becoming crowded when, as spring came on, our children brought in toads, salamanders, turtles, snakes and other pets.

I drove the owls to the country one morning when the time seemed ripe and liberated them in the woods. I hoped that they would find things more challenging there than in the library that was something of a welfare state.

* * * * * * * * * *

Great Horned Owls, for all their power and, at times, ferocity, have hootings as mild as the cooings of Mourning Doves. Thoreau was doubtless referring to Barred Owls when he wrote of hootings as being "idiotic and maniacal." The regular hootings of these owls, far from bizarre, are a "who, hoo, hoo-hoo" that is easy to imitate. On occasions, however, Barred Owls make a cacophony of "whos" and "who-ahs" that well fit Thoreau's description. These caterwaulings, heard suddenly in the middle of a dark night as Jane and I heard them outside of our bedroom window in Bethesda, are truly maniacal, even blood-curdling.

I have heard friends describe terrible noises, heard when camping, that they fancied might be catamounts or even bears fighting. It has seemed to Jane and me that they were more likely listening to the caterwaulings of Barred Owls, one of the most startling sounds made by any bird or animal. Why should the owls make such noises?

If one can judge from studies made of the related Tawny Owl in England, individuals or pairs of owls hurl their maniacal caterwauls back and forth to establish territorial boundaries. This fits to some extent with Jane's and my experience. In South Carolina, when staying by a cypress swamp where Barred Owls were common, we heard caterwauls almost nightly. In Maryland and New Hampshire, on the other hand, where the owls are widely scattered, we have heard caterwauling very infrequently—only three times in eight years in Bethesda.

But I do not think that the caterwauls are entirely territorial. While they probably evolved for this func-

tion, they may have acquired an additional use associated with the death of grey squirrels. Is this too
bizarre an idea?

Now I am far from being a Charles Darwin or even
a Sherlock Holmes, but I have had two experiences
that have set me thinking. Why should one not try to
reason from what one has noted in nature? Is not this
part of the enjoyment of natural history?

The first experience was with a mother squirrel in
our yard. While many are frustrated by squirrels, my
philosophy is "if you can't lick'em, join'em." With
this in mind I converted ours into pets. I often sat on
our back porch before going to work to feed them
raw peanuts. They came to my lap and I got to know
them individually. I was not at all disturbed when
boxes I had put up on poles for flickers were appro-
priated by the squirrels.

I heard a strange noise in the yard one dark night.
Taking a flashlight I stepped outside. In the beam of
my light was a mother squirrel heading for one of the
flicker boxes, a baby squirrel in her teeth, its body
wrapped like a collar around her neck. I had not
realized before this that grey squirrels could move
about in the dark.

It was some nights later that Jane and I were shaken out of sleep by the "whoos" and "who-ahs" of a
Barred Owl caterwauling in our small yard.

The next day I saw no sign of the mother squirrel.
But this was not unusual for mother squirrels are
secretive when with young. I forgot about her for
several days when I noticed something peculiar at the
squirrel box. Half-grown young were lolling at the
entrance and one had fallen to the ground. They
were thin and emaciated. What had happened to the
mother?

I collected the young ones and brought them to Jane in the kitchen. She soon had them nursing on a baby bottle and once fed, she carried them about in apron pockets where they felt secure.

These matters settled, I again thought of the mother squirrel. Why should she have disappeared on the night of the caterwauling? Could there have been a connection?

Could the owl have been celebrating a successful hunt? But this idea seemed unreasonable. Intrigued, I read what I could find about Barred Owls and their prey.

As I had suspected from their comparatively weak talons, Barred Owls live primarily on mice, young rabbits being considered as being the largest prey they can seize effectively. Would not a full-grown squirrel be more than they could handle?

A Great Horned Owl, swooping down on a squirrel or even a skunk three-times larger, would strike a blow so paralyzing that the animal would have little chance to struggle before it was dead. I am well acquainted with the power of the talons of Great Horneds from handling Bo.

But a Barred Owl swooping on a squirrel under similar circumstances, would encounter difficulties. Would not the squirrel struggle and thrash about? It was this point that I pondered. Supposing the owl let go with a blood-curdling caterwaul the moment it struck, might not the squirrel, suddenly and overwhelmingly terrified, go into a state of shock? Audiogenic seizures have been demonstrated among laboratory animals. Why should they not take place in nature? Noise machines have, I understand, been designed as weapons to lay the enemy low in modern

war. Could not caterwauling be used as a similar de-
vice for subduing prey?

* * * * * * * * * *

I had little occasion to think of these ideas for some
years. We had moved to New Hampshire and had few
encounters with Barred Owls there. Then one winter's day the telephone rang. I was sitting at lunch at
the medical school at Hanover. At the other end of
the line was a much excited lady. She had been driving by the college park at Dartmouth when she saw an
owl on the snow by the street, screaming like "ten
thousand Blue Jays." What was the matter? Was it
hurt?

Thanking the lady for the call, I grabbed my field
glasses and left the medical school on the run. The
park was just across the street.

Luck was with me. When I reached the place the
lady had referred to, a Barred Owl rose from the
snow bearing a large grey squirrel. The squirrel was
obviously about all the owl could carry. It barely
cleared the snow.

The snow was fresh and I ran to the spot from
whence the owl had flown. There was an impression
where the squirrel had lain, but no signs of blood or
fur and no signs of a struggle. But there were burrows showing that the squirrel had been active close
by, digging under the snow for acorns and spruce
cones.

For a Barred Owl to be caterwauling over a territorial boundary by a busy street at mid-day, and killing
a squirrel at the same time seemed unlikely. Could
there be something to my theory about caterwauling
as a weapon after all?

* * * * * * * * * *

I wrote up my ideas in scientific form and submitted them to a professional bird journal. "Expect little, enjoy much" said Goethe. I did not flatter myself that my note would be accepted for publication but I enjoyed writing it.

I received the verdicts of two experts some months later. The first was brief and adamant. The note was not worth publishing because it had no evidence. A second expert was more kindly (and more imaginative). He thought the idea an excellent one for research and he was glad to have it. Would I send him a reprint when it was published?

Needless to say the reaction of the latter expert was most pleasing. This was not just because he had reacted favorably to my theory. If Charles Darwin could say that he never had a first formed hypothesis that he did not have to change later, should I not be wary of taking too much stock in mine? What I liked about the second expert was that he said 'yes' to a new idea.

What evidence did Columbus have for his theory when he set sail? Life, I feel, belongs to the adventurous. It is a joy to observe and to experience nature. It is also a joy to try to make sense of what one sees. Said Sir Francis Darwin of his father "He often said that no one could be a good observer unless he was an active theoriser." No higher degrees are needed for this. Darwin had none and liked to think of himself as being only a naturalist.

* * * * * * * * * *

Thoreau died too soon to have read Darwin. His thoughts flowed along different lines. When writing of owls, he considered their hootings as being "idiotic and maniacal," expressing the "infinite roominess of nature." Actually it seems more probable that the caterwauls of Barred Owls express the parceling out of nature into territories. Also, if my theory has any value, they may represent a strategm for subduing large prey, rather than being just maniacal.

But I have never been willing to let myself be swamped by science. There is room for a Charles Darwin and a Thoreau. The sounds of nature are thrilling; they penetrate best without too much analysis. I like to lay aside theories when I go to the woods and to be open to what I see and hear, something that is not difficult when it comes to listening to the hootings of Barred and other owls.

XVII. ENJOYING (AND LEARNING FROM) A TAME PILEATED

"Each time I study a new species I am amazed to find how much more I see after I have become thoroughly acquainted with it."–N. Tinbergen.

I have had ambitions in regard to birds. Among those unrealized, were visions of a library with windows opening into aviaries, made attractive with growing plants and each containing a pair of birds that would breed and raise young where I could watch them from day to day.

In a prominent place would have been the pair of Black and White Casqued Hornbills that we had hand-raised and brought from Africa; in another Blue Jays, in others pairs of Red-bellied, Hairy and other woodpeckers; White-breasted Nuthatches and finally, as my *pièce de résistance,* a pair of Pileated Woodpeckers. Had I started earlier, I might have accomplished all of these things.

By way of compensation I think that our indoor garage, made over into an aviary, had its merits. It was manageable and I had a chance to get to know my woodpeckers well. I was left with freedom for hours in the woods as well as having time before going to work in the morning or after coming home in the evening to enjoy my birds. Of these, none was more enjoyable than Silly Pilly, our female Pileated Woodpecker.

A ridiculous name? Perhaps. But of the two Pileateds we have had for any length of time, both had a Donald Duck appearance when seen head-on, due to the widths of their mouths and the benign friendly look in their eyes. Silly Pilly was merely a term of endearment. If one wants to make progress with animals, I feel with Fraser Darling that one should regard them as "likeable children of our own kind." Any name is suitable if it puts one in the right frame of mind.

When I first saw the female Pileated and her brother in southern Florida one day in May, they looked anything but promising. I had found a pair of Pileateds nesting 50 feet up in a dead pine that seemed too slender to accommodate the nest of so large a bird. Climbing to such a nest would have been impossible.

I was fortunately staying at the Archbold Biological Station and was able to get the help of two men, ropes and an extension ladder. The plan was to cut the tree, then lower it gently with ropes. All worked well except that in lowering the dead pine it became entangled with a living one. The ladder was put up and I climbed to the nest hole to take out a pair of baby Pileateds. They were mostly naked, with pin feathers just starting to appear.

What astonished me was that the walls of their nest consisted of only a half-inch of rotten wood and bark. The next strong wind might have broken the dead pine at the level of the nest, exposing the young to the elements. It was consoling to think that my taking them may have saved their lives.

I set out for our home in Maryland the next morning. The woodpeckers were so small that I carried them aboard the plane in a paper bag without attracting attention.

When Jane and I looked in on them the following morning they flattened down and hissed like snakes. I had never seen this frightening behavior before excepting once with flickers and once with young Hairies. Like the flickers, the two Pileateds became tame in no time. We only saw the hissing behavior twice again. Once was when our maid, Alberta, looked in at them for the first time. The other was when we took the lid from their box too abruptly.

The nestlings took food readily. I found a section of hollow log that made a somewhat natural type of nest. Within a few days the Pileateds were using wings and feet to clamber up the sides in what Jane called the "elevator system." Once fed at the top, a youngster would drop to the bottom. Here the two, their stomachs filled, would start contented jabbering and "peep-peep-peep" notes as we covered them over. Eat and sleep, eat and sleep!

When nearly half-grown the male gave a series of "cuks, cuk, cuks," and some days later began to preen his emerging feathers.

I was away for a week soon after the Pileateds left their nest and during that time the male died. One learns the hard way in raising birds!

The female, to our relief, remained in fine shape. She called "cuks" when I entered the house and flew to eat from my fingers when I approached the aviary. Afterward she ran her long tongue, flickering like a flamethrower, over the creases and buttons of my denim jacket.

When she came to my left side, she started pounding with her bill. I think the pulsations of my heart made her think that a large larva lay underneath— one needing to be dug out. I felt perhaps it was the same "pulsations in a tube" sound experienced by a Hairy Woodpecker in the aviary when it struck at arteries under my scalp.

By the time Pilly was eight weeks old she played dodgeball every morning, fluttering her wings and shifting about on the underside of a slanting log as if facing an enemy. It was the game played by the Hairy, Downy, and others of my captive woodpeckers. But Pilly remained the most playful of them all, often circling the aviary in a wild, looping flight after the dodgeball.

I enjoyed watching these demonstrations of health and exuberance. Pilly was one of the most affectionate and playful of woodpeckers. She treated Jane and me as if we were ones of her own kind, and gave "cuks" in the excitement of seeing us enter the room.

When two months old she became interested in a female Yellow-bellied Sapsucker, pointing her bill and waving it in a swinging motion as she half-started her wings in a dance used by Pileateds in courtship. At the same time she gave pleasing "woick, woicks". At other times she would hop toward the sapsucker, her bill held up at 45 degrees. The smaller bird never returned these advances. Indeed she seemed quite unnoticing.

Wanting to be sure as to the source of the Pileated's behavior, I removed the sapsucker from the aviary for several days. The Pileated became quiet immediately. When I reintroduced the sapsucker, Pilly responded with what, to this onlooker, was great rejoicing. She flew to the smaller bird with crest raised, giving the most effusive set of "woicks" and bill-wavings that I had seen. There was no doubt about her attachment to the smaller bird.

One may ask why this special attraction to the sapsucker and not to the other woodpeckers? It was, perhaps, because a female sapsucker looks to some extent like a miniature male Pileated. Both have red crests and white throats as well as black and white bands radiating from the base of the bill. Of all the woodpeckers in the aviary, the sapsucker had the best set of releasers for a female Pileated.

If I had not read Konrad Lorenz's famous paper on "Companions as factors in the bird's environment," I might have found the antics of a Pileated displaying to a sapsucker puzzling. One might think from such behavior that birds are very different from human beings. But is this true? Who has not seen the devotion of a lone female of *Homo sapiens* to a cat, a lap dog, or even a horse? The need of a love object is far from being confined to birds.

Pilly made love, but only briefly, with one other woodpecker in the aviary—a male Red-bellied Woodpecker looking nothing like a sapsucker. But he did have head feathers of the same silky texture and flaming red color as those in the crests of Pileated Woodpeckers. Pilly made "woicks" and bill-wavings to the Red-belly as soon as the latter had molted into his adult plumage. Unlike the sapsucker, the Red-belly responded. But the response was not one of affection.

What he saw in the flaming crest of the female Pileated was apparently a rival male of his own kind and one of superoptimal proportions! Pilly was soon releasing not love but aggressiveness. Unable to meet the Red-belly's incessant attacks, Silly Pilly took refuge in her roost box and would have remained there for days had I not removed her tormentor.

It was not enough to put the Red-belly in an adjoining cage. He kept trying to attack through the wire. I had to build a small aviary out of sight at the back of the house before peace was restored.

A big event in the life of the Pileated that autumn was the adoption of a roost box. She had been spending nights hanging to the turkey wire, close under the ceiling. To enter a dark roost hole was, for her, like taking a plunge into a dark pool. She was most hesitant. For some days she kept looking in with obvious interest but indecision. Finally she entered, came out and re-entered. A milestone had been passed!

The roost box was a piece of hollow log bearing a patchwork of tin and aluminum as protection against blows of her bill. It now became a place of refuge and solace. She drove other woodpeckers away from it, even the female sapsucker.

One of Pilly's occupations was to drum on the inside of the roost box—not a regular kind of drumming, but rather a rapid series of small drum taps. It sounded like an old fashioned sewing machine in the way it started and stopped, so much so that it fooled our young son completely. He was sure that someone must be at the sewing machine.

Another curious noise was her tongue rattle. This was made by the horny tip of Pilly's tongue as it ran over surfaces and crevices of dry wood. The sound was something like that of a rattlesnake.

All the time I watched by the aviary I learned little things. This was not because Pilly was changing her performances, for her daily routines were often much the same. But I had opportunities to observe some aspects of behavior repeatedly, ones giving insight into the ways of woodpeckers.

Each morning, usually after some playful dodging, Pilly would stretch, scratch, and preen. How humdrum, one might say. Yet even here I learned of features that no one had described before as far as I was aware.

A great many birds lower one wing, then raise the foot between it and the body to scratch the head. Yet morning after morning Pilly scratched her head directly with no movement of her wing. So did the other woodpeckers in the aviary.

Birds commonly extend one wing way down and out in stretching, with the leg of the same side extending with it. But Pilly and the other woodpeckers moved the wing out with both feet remaining in place. I watched this closely day after day. There were exceptions. One was when the Pileated was on an insecure perch and the leg had to be moved to retain balance. Another, perhaps related, was when the young Pileateds were at the age of nest-leaving. It is possible that they were unsteady at that time as well.

Sometimes bits of behavior were brought out unexpectedly. One could never anticipate just what would upset the woodpeckers. I entered the aviary one morning to wash the windows. Pilly was much distressed, rapping "bam, bam" with her bill as she eyed me from the top of a log. It was a good display of the actions of a Pileated when disturbed. I had seen a similar performance when standing too close to roost holes of wild Pileateds in the evening.

Another phenomenon seen at close range was the way Pilly used her long, flexible tongue. She was fond of bits of toast. If I brought her a piece roughly a quarter by three-eighths of an inch in size it would be too large for her to handle and she would be helpless.

This situation was not true for the other wood-peckers. The Hairy, the sapsucker, or the Red-belly always took an object too large to handle to an anvil or some crevice, then pounded it into smaller pieces. They would catch crumbs by pushing their bellies against the log below while bringing the bends of their folded wings forward.

Pilly could not do this, seeming to lack instinct for the performance. This was possibly because Pileateds live largely on ants. They also eat large grubs, but these, being smooth and cylindrical, may be easy to swallow without prior pounding.

I liked to place a piece of toast of the right size nearly beyond Pilly's reach, about four inches outside of the turkey wire. Pilly would then flick her tongue way out, over two inches beyond her bill, curl it neatly on the far side, then flick the morsel deftly to where she could reach it with her bill.

It is this kind of thing that one cannot see in the wild. Yet all the time one watches Pileateds their long tongues are performing remarkable maneuvers deep inside logs and stumps. Thus day by day I felt that I was building up details about Pileateds.

There was one small vocalization that Pilly made when working over logs in the aviary. This was a low "hn, hn" noise. Sometimes, when given more loudly, it reminded me of the "gw-un, gw-un" notes made by scolding grey squirrels. I have heard these notes made by wild Pileateds as they fed close to one another. It may be a way of keeping in touch or expressing awareness of each other's proximity. Such notes are made by many kinds of birds with close pair bonds.

Possibly Pilly felt a close association to Jane and me. We hoped so. As Konrad Lorenz said in "King Solomon's Ring," "it is a wonderful thing to feel a bond with some other creature . . . to have a sense of understanding."

Each summer I put Pilly into a small cage, loaded her into our Jeep, and drove her and our other woodpeckers from Maryland to our summer place in New Hampshire. She seemed to ride well with the cage covered. At the journey's end I transferred her to an aviary built of turkey wire on a back porch. Pilly almost never gave high calls in Maryland but she gave them repeatedly in New Hampshire in response to wild Pileateds living in woods nearby.

Other wild creatures lived there also. Jane and I learned of this when we were awakened one night by piercing screams. I jumped up and ran to the aviary. What I found was a large raccoon on the outside of the cage attacking as well as being attacked by the Pileated. The racoon jumped to the ground and ran off. Pilly had a hard time quieting down. Even five minutes later she still kept flying to the wire with wings outspread, as if the raccoon were still there.

I then returned to bed, a futile move. Within a short time we were awakened by another set of cries. This time I found Pilly, what was left of her, still striking at her adversary the raccoon. I almost had to drive the 'coon away to make him let go of Pilly, whose feathers littered the floor. Our woodpecker looked like a plucked chicken, one leg dangling and broken. I despaired for her life. What hope could there be? Jane, fortunately, felt more confident and was able to tape the broken leg into a metal splint while I held the bird on the kitchen table.

Our Pileated was a model patient throughout her period of helplessness, allowing us to feed her by hand as if she had reverted to being a nestling. For the first week she clung motionless to the side of her cage. By nine days she made slight movements with her injured leg and began preening and giving high calls whenever wild Pileateds came to the edge of the clearing. Her response to us remained most trusting.

Even after 18 days we could handle and feed her with ease. At the end of this time I returned to Maryland, leaving Pilly with Jane and children. By the time I returned six weeks later, Pilly was completely restored and looking as good as new. The only real loss from the raccoon was that on another night it succeeded in killing Pilly's companion, the female sapsucker.

* * * * * * * * * *

One might ask in retrospect why the Pileated should have let herself be caught. The aviary was nine feet across and seven feet high. She had plenty of room to keep away, yet she had flown at and attacked the raccoon deliberately. My feeling is that under natural circumstances a Pileated Woodpecker would never meet a raccoon or other intruder except face to face at the entrance to a roost or nest hole. There, protected by cavity walls and striking out through the entrance, a combative spirit might be effective. Even a large raccoon might not be able to cope with the jabbing blows of a Pileated's bill directed at its snout and eyes at close range. The instinct for Pilly to attack, therefore, was possibly not so foolish as it appeared. Her roosting in an open cage was unnatural.

* * * * * * * * * *

When we moved to New Hampshire and Dartmouth in 1961 I had so many problems to contemplate in getting settled that I felt forced to give up the aviary. I let some of the birds go and gave others to the zoo. It was several years before we had settled sufficiently to build aviaries in our new home and to start again.

The prospect of getting another Pileated seemed slim. Wild Pileateds are widely scattered in Lyme, where we live, and nests difficult to find. But in mid-June of 1968 I found one in an aspen near a dirt road. The young had their heads out of the hole and would be leaving in a few days. How could I ever reach them, 50 feet up?

I remembered having seen some tree surgeons at work alongside the main highway. Within an hour a young man with climbing irons was at the hole. He put the two nestlings in a cloth bag and lowered them down. What a prize! I had a male and a female, the latter the older and larger of the two. (A peculiarity of young Pileateds, as distinct from nestling Hairies, Downies, flickers, or sapsuckers, is that one can tell the sexes apart, even in the nest).

I soon had the two in a hollow log nest box. Their cries were harsh on being fed, but I had heard the same sounds when their parents had come to the aspen. Of the two, the female was the most advanced. When I put my face close, she pecked gently at the rim of my glasses, then flicked her long tongue over my eyebrows. Within two days she flew from her artificial nest and was a nestling no longer.

Her brother was not ready to leave until 48 hours later. He still made continuous noises, like those of a grey squirrel when taking food from my fingers. When I stopped by the hollow log nest in the middle of the night, I heard him making soft up and down "who-whoos" suggesting an owl. Could these suggestive imitations of rival hole-nesters have meanings? I wish I knew.

Our young woodpeckers seemed to delight in making a variety of noises. Perhaps, to them, it was a form of play or a way of learning. Woodpeckers make certain vocalizations, such as the whinny and high call that are unvarying. In courtship they utter other sounds of considerable variety. Perhaps, again, an element of play comes in and the parent-young relation is revived between the members of a pair. The lives of birds are less stereotyped and more variable than many are willing to believe.

My new Pileateds were delightful. The female was tame from the start, greeting me with "chuck, qu-uck" notes mixed with "cuks" whenever I came in sight.

She and her brother spent their first week hanging close to the ceiling of their aviary, exploring every-thing within reach of their long tongues. Silent when by themselves, their vocalizations were loudest when we came to feed them their assorted diet of baby mice, hamburger and meal worms. When I held the female on my hand she attacked my wrist watch, pos-sibly thinking there was some kind of insect ticking inside.

The Pileateds remained quiet when alone but, after ten days, began to greet us with high calls. I had been following a family of wild Pileateds in the woods and noted that the wild juveniles also gave high calls. This pleased me. I felt reassured that what we observed in the aviary had a foundation in nature.

In July Jane found a baby Blue Jay in the woods. It was too young to fly and had seemingly fallen from its nest. We placed the bird in the aviary, naming her Jazy.

The male Pileated paid no attention. The female reacted by approaching the newcomer with aggres-sive threat displays, opening her wings way out. Even three days later she made the same threats, raising and lowering her crest and striking—fortunately in a harmless manner—at the helpless jay.

Meanwhile Jazy was learning. We saw her practis-ing a flight of three feet across the floor of the aviary and she kept practising. The Pileateds did not intimi-date her at all.

* * * * * * * * *

One always has to face a certain number of tragedies with hand-raised birds. Why we lost the female Pileated in July I have no idea. The male remained in splendid shape and in lieu of his sister had Jazy as his companion.

When in the woods I noticed a rock maple with a furrow of rotten wood, as though it had once been struck by lightning. I brought home a six foot section of the trunk, setting it up in the aviary for the Pileated. He seemed to take delight in the log, running his long tongue into its various holes and crevices. This was just a prelude to striking powerful blows that, after several hours of work, left a series of deep pits in the furrow.

Jazy, meanwhile, perched a foot away. Anything new excited her and she sang full blast, with a variety of tunes of her own composition. Occasionally she caught an insect scared up by the Pileated. Sometimes she would play with a splinter he had let loose. The Pileated, engrossed in his carpentry, paid little attention to the jay aside from occasionally poking at and nearly touching her with his tongue.

By September the Pileated had the look of an adult. His shoulders had broadened, his crest was a flaming red. The rest of his plumage was black with a nice sheen to it. His eyes now had yellow coming into them, contributing to a fierce, wild look. He was a magnificent specimen.

I took to bringing a chair into the aviary at lunch time, so that I could have more time to look at him. Early in September Jazy, who had never brought me anything before, placed a toothpick on my lunch plate, an act that seemed so deliberate I wondered if she knew I would like it. She then whistled one of her songs with much enthusiasm.

Meanwhile the Pileated clung to the wire close by, contemplating the two of us. When he made some low "wuck, wuck" notes, Jazy immediately mimicked them. With much further talk-talk she pulled at my shirt collar, then stuck her bill into my mouth. As I looked over at the Pileated staring at us, I was again reminded of the Donald Duck look these birds can have when seen head on.

A week later I opened the window and gave Jazy her freedom. She went out onto the limbs of a nearby tree, whistling and singing a conglomerate of notes that included the "cuk-cuk-cuks" and "wuck, wucks" of the Pileated Woodpecker.

A few days later I let the Pileated go. How magnificent he looked in the open; flaming crest, yellow eyes, and his large size! He moved away slowly, looking fully competent to care for himself. I supposed that if we were to meet in the woods later on he would be as shy of me as any other of his kind.

But what about Jazy? Would she know, with her powers of imitation, how to speak to him with "cuk, cuks" and "wuck, wucks" he might understand? It was pleasant to think that of the three of us that had shared lunch hours, at least two of the group might meet again.

Since liberation of the Pileated Jane and I have kept other birds only briefly. For 16 years on and off we had kept a considerable number, but looking after birds is a confining occupation.

We, like Jazy and the Pileated at the end of their first summer, reached the time when we wanted our freedom . . . in our case to travel to southlands in search of new adventures, with no pets needing to be fed tying us to home.

XVIII. KINGFISHERS IN THE GARDEN

"It is only by living with animals that one can attain a real understanding of their ways."–Konrad Lorenz.

Kingfishers are spectacular birds to have in one's garden. The experiences that Jane and I had occurred in opposite corners of the world, the first in equatorial Africa and the second, at our home in Lyme, New Hampshire.

In 1954 and '55 my wife, five small children and I were living in Entebbe, Uganda, our house being within the compound of the Virus Research Institute. The garden was unbelievably attractive to birds—too many to watch them all. There was everything from hornbills to hoopoes. My special interest came to be in the hornbills and the Woodland Kingfisher.

Woodland Kingfishers are beautiful birds with vermilion bills and cobalt blue plumages trimmed with jet black. Ours had an entrancing song: "Ka-chrr-rr-wree-ee-oo-oo" that rang out in early morning hours. One of the kingfisher's extraordinary performances was bathing. A kingfisher would perch 20 feet above a bird bath then, as many as eight times in 15 minutes, plunge headlong into water a mere three inches deep.

There was a dead tree with two holes in it outside our bedroom window.

We soon discovered that the kingfishers were house-hunting and were much interested. In this they were not alone. Other hole-nesting birds gave signs that they, too, found the tree holes attractive. But the kingfishers were tyrants and competitors had little chance.

One day a pair of Grey Woodpeckers, about the size of Downies, tried to edge near the smaller of the two holes. One of the kingfishers came after the male like a bullet. We saw little of the woodpeckers thereafter, even though they had possibly made the hole in the first place. Other hole-nesters, including Long-tailed Glossy Starlings and a Double-toothed Barbet, fared no better.

One kingfisher or the other would occasionally cling to the bark of the larger hole looking in. We had no way of identifying the sexes at this stage, for the birds were similar in plumage. Yet it was obvious they were preparing to nest.

As days passed the singing increased. The male fed his mate a sizeable grasshopper at the hole. She came out and the two perched quietly side by side. Mating followed. Later one of them raised its wings and spread them out in what I supposed was courtship.

By November the kingfishers were feeding their young with grasshoppers and sometimes with cockroaches about two inches long. A parent kingfisher would sling a cockroach sideways in its bill to subdue it in the same manner that water kingfishers sling a fish.

* * * * * * * * * *

The walk from our house to the institute was a delightful one through gardens and under flowering trees. As I walked along one morning I saw a Pied Crow attacking some smaller bird. I ran fast to frighten the crow before it could fly off with its prey. The victim was one of our Woodland Kingfishers. I supposed it had struck a neighboring building or wire for it seemed unlikely that the crow could have caught it otherwise. The kingfisher was giving its last gasps as I picked it up. What would happen to its young?

By six that evening Jane and I had seen no activity at the nest and the nestlings were clamoring for food. I called for Mike, our ten-year-old son, and we set up a ladder. Mike climbed up, took out three young birds still in pinfeathers and handed them down. Looking back in the nest he found the bottom lined with wings of large cockroaches.

Jane and I were raising a Long-tailed Glossy Starling at the time and we soon had the young kingfishers feeding on the same diet of pilchards rolled in baby food.

By the end of a week the young kingfishers were waddling about on their short legs, begging lustily for cockroaches when we had them. At other times they had to get along on chilled honey bees. These may seem a strange food but we had laid by a store when Africans from the institute removed a bees' nest from the roof.

When stuffed with chilled bees and cockroaches, the nestlings crowded together in a corner—cozily laying heads and necks across one another.

Less than two weeks later the largest of the kingfishers—they had apparently hatched on different days and hence were not all of the same size— refused to beg, but seized a cockroach from my fingers. After a few minutes of vigorous swallowing aided by flappings of wings, the kingfisher downed its prey.

Three days later the youngsters were flying up and down the screened corridor leading to our bedroom. With kingfishers and the starling we were on our way to having a fine aviary.

* * * * * * * * * *

There were other species of kingfishers about Entebbe, which is a peninsula jutting into Lake Victoria. The Striped Kingfisher came to the institute compound after the Woodland Kingfishers had gone. One was usually perched on a telephone wire when, pointing its bill upward and briefly extending its wings, it called its "pee-yrr, pee-yrr" over and over. The notes became a familiar sound.

Another tiny land kingfisher was the Pygmy I found perched on a wire fence. It repeatedly shot down to the grass for prey, then returned right back to where it had come from.

The Pied Kingfisher was one of the most common and conspicuous birds along the lake shore. One could see dozens of them at a time, hovering over the water for fish. Many nested in holes dug in a cattle pasture at the end of the peninsula.

To see the beautiful Malacite Kingfisher one had to hire a native canoe. Then, gliding along the bay that lay below the institute, one might see an occasional one of these tiny gems along the wall of papyrus.

What opportunities for the study of kingfishers Entebbe offered! I did not progress far, but I did get an idea of their variety. This proved a useful background when, nearly 20 years later, Jane and I raised three young Belted Kingfishers in New Hampshire.

* * * * * * * * *

The Belted Kingfishers arrived by accident one 28th of June when a lady at the medical school asked if I would like some young woodpeckers. Workmen, she said, had been hauling gravel from a bank when the three young birds tumbled from a burrow. Incredible, I thought. Were these flickers perhaps nesting like ground woodpeckers? Great was my surprise when, looking into a paper bag, I saw three young kingfishers—the woodpeckers of my unornithological friend.

The nestlings were of different sizes and had obviously hatched on different days. The youngest made a trill when hungry, but the two oldest were silent. A peculiar effect of the trill was to make me feel my ear drums moving in and out, a sensation I have had with no other sound.

The nestlings swallowed minnows and, when we ran out of these, strips of raw fish. We kept the birds in a Dutch oven by the fireplace thinking they would like the dark. When I opened the oven door the white spots in front of their eyes stood out prominently. I wondered if the spots served to guide parents, enabling them to orient their young at the end of the dark burrow that forms the natural nest. The young, in turn, might orient to a parent's white spots in seeking a meal.

Later observations on the kingfishers fell into three stages: first when they were in a "nest" consisting of a plastic basin with straw in the bottom, placed in a large carton that could be darkened; second when, after fledging on July 9, they were kept in an aviary for 10 days; and thirdly the time they remained in the yard, following their liberation on July 19.

* * * * * * * * * *

Those who have opened kingfisher burrows in nature have found them surprisingly clean, although parents are not known to carry away fecal matter. Cornwell (1963), who kept young Belted Kingfishers in much the same manner as we did, noted that they used corners as latrines, rapping on the walls above in a way that would have covered over the excreta.

It seemed to us that these ideas needed modification. Our kingfishers ejected fecal matter with such force that it went over the edge of the wash basin "nest" and spattered the walls—not in any corner, but in all directions. While holding a young kingfisher on one's finger, one could see the excreta travel out for a distance of several feet, an untidy performance when it landed on the library rug.

This ejection was restricted to the nestling stage. Why should the young have such a propulsive mechanism? Were they open-nesters, like hawks, the propulsion would carry their droppings over the rim of the nest and keep it clean. But in a small chamber, deep in a sand bank, this would be impossible.

Our idea was that the exreta of young kingfishers adheres to sand or dirt walls under natural conditions, explaining the curious habit our nestlings had of rapping on the walls of their box. One might presume the effect would be to wear down the crumbly walls of a nest chamber. This process would fit descriptions of nests as being circular as well as clean. (Yet not entirely clean for the young cast up pellets of fish scales, bones and other solid matter.)

* * * * * * * * * *

A friend and critic on reading the above details wondered whether I should not soften my remarks on the exreta of our birds. Had not Jane and I become too callous about such matters, after years of raising young of many kinds? Might not someone be offended?

I confess that I become carried away by natural history. Nest sanitation can be of vital importance in survival, for sloppiness of even a slight degree may be enough to betray a nest to a predator. I am content, therefore, to record what I see leaving Jane, as happens at times, to clean up the messes afterward.

Were I a more accomplished writer, like the Elizabethan poet, scholar and wit Sir John Harrington, I might accomplish things more delicately. According to Lytton Strachey, Sir John was so offended by sanitary arrangements in the houses of the great that he was inspired to invent the water-closet.

"Then seizing his pen, he concocted a pamphlet after the manner of Rabelais—or, as he preferred to call him 'the Reverent Rabbles'—in which extravagant spirits, intolerable puns, improper stories, and sly, satirical digs at eminent personages were blended together into a preposterous rhapsody, followed by an appendix—written, of course, by his servant—could a gentleman be expected to discuss such deatils?—containing a minute account, with measurements, diagrams and prices, of the invention."

We are told further that Queen Elizabeth, "with her supreme sense of the practical, saw that—'the marrow of the book' was not entirely ludicrous." She sent down word to the poet that she approved of his contrivance and was having one installed in Richmond Palace.

Belted Kingfishers, too, have developed contrivances. I only wish that I had the pen of a Sir John Harrington to do more justice to their arrangements—developed, no doubt, over centuries of natural selection.

* * * * * * * * * *

Our growing kingfishers were soon able to handle comparatively large items such as commercial smelt. The youngest often swallowed two in succession, enormous amounts for a bird of his size. The two older ones ate less as they approached the time of fledging.

Our nestlings chittered, preened and stretched their wings and tails as well as eating and sleeping. They also made flying motions by extending their wings, vibrating, then pressing them down to lift their bodies upward. Sometimes the oldest pulled its head up and down in giving a rattle like an adult.

One kingfisher or another would occasionally pick up a piece of straw, clamp its bill along it, then playfully sling the straw sideways as though it were a freshly caught fish. Were the youngsters practising, in play, habits that might be of use later on?

The female flew from the cardboard carton and circled the library 12 days after we had acquired her. This was a great occasion. Her nestling days were over.

We now put the three kingfishers in an aviary in the greenhouse, thinking it time they graduated from the cardboard box. They perched demurely in their new abode for the next five days taking food every two to three hours.

We placed a plastic pool stocked with goldfish and minnows at the bottom of the aviary. The kingfishers took no interest in feeding themselves at first. Then on July 16 I found the female all wet. The next day one of the four goldfish in the pool was missing. From that day on all the tadpoles and fish placed in the pool disappeared. I was never able to see a kingfisher dive after them until I hid myself and watched, for our birds were becoming increasingly wild.

On July 19 the female dove from a shelf seven feet up, caught a newt and returned to her perch. She clamped on it a few times, then discarded it. Newts seemed to be distasteful and I did not try them again.

The older male dove with more success and caught a green frog tadpole, beat it sideways and swallowed it. It was a pleasure to see that our hand-raised birds were becoming able to care for themselves. The aviary was now too small and I took the birds outdoors one late afternoon, to give them their liberty. They flew off, only to return by evening to roost on the roof of the house.

We moved the plastic pool from the aviary to a place·on the lawn. Would the kingfishers return? At noon the next day the female flew into the yard, alighted at the edge of the woodshed roof and studied the pool. Jane and I were then thrilled to see her dive 20 feet, hit the water with a splash, and emerge with a tadpole. Our hopes for kingfishers in the garden were realized!

Shortly afterward the youngest kingfisher dove for a dead commercial smelt. He was possibly too young to go after live prey. We had fledged him prematurely.

I noticed several times that the juvenile kingfishers might swim to the edge of the pool by flapping with their wings, after diving, as though unable to fly up from the water.

Kingfisher-watching now became an exciting sport. Whenever we heard a rattle, or saw a flash of blue, we rushed to the door. A dive from the roof, a splash, a bird arising with its struggling prey—these were our rewards. We had set the stage and things were working beyond expectations.

There is an account in Bent's Life Histories of how parent kingfishers teach their young to fish. Details given are few and I decided from watching our birds that the fishing is instinctive and requires no parental help.

It is possible, nonetheless, that parents teach their young some things. On July 21 the female spent more than two hours resting on the top of a five-foot post that I had placed by the pool. When our cat came by and reached up toward her, she showed no alarm. Possibly in nature, warning cries from a parent might have taught her what animals are to be feared.

* * * * * * * * *

Kingfishers are solitary birds, spacing themselves along streams and lake shores. This may explain why ours never became pets in the manner of the more social jays and crows we had raised under similar circumstances.

The kingfishers had been peaceful with each other when indoors. But once in the yard they never associated and on July 21 I saw the female attack the youngest male, opening her bill an inch at the tip as she did so.

The trouble with our experiment in the garden was that our birds learned too fast and became independent too soon. The female left us after four days and the youngest after seven.

Was this the last we would see of them? I thought so until a week later when I began to notice a smallish kingfisher by a waterfall and pool a mile away. Some boys who swam there had strung a rope across. Week after week, through August and into September, I saw the kingfisher perched on the rope. If it was our youngest, it had found an attractive spot to stay.

* * * * * * * * *

The African experience gave me thoughts about our birds in Lyme. One question was why should Belted Kingfishers have small, prominent white spots between eyes and the base of the bill? Others of the larger fish-eating kingfishers, such as the Pied and Ringed, have similar white spots or lines. The land or insect-eating kingfishers that we saw in our Entebbe garden, on the other hand, did not.

A thought is that the white spots gather light, serving to guide vision along grooves in the upper mandible, as one might sight a gun on a target. This is not needed for land kingfishers that see their prey directly. The fish-catchers, on the contrary, have to make a correction—one allowing for the refraction of water. Otherwise they would overshoot the mark.

It is of interest that the European Kingfisher, that may be representative of aquatic kingfishers in general, has two centers of acute vision in its retina: one for air and the other for water. Possibly sighting along the bill aids in switching from one to the other.

These musings are questions I cannot answer, but of one thing I am certain. Watching hand-raised birds such as our kingfishers gives one a sense of close acquaintance. Questions arise and one becomes—or so one hopes—better able to observe and discover on later occasions.

As Robert Louis Stevenson remarked, "though I sink many times beneath the waves, yet am I upborne by the spirit of discovery." I suppose a kingfisher would write that "though I sink many times, yet am I upborne by the fun of catching another fish."

I like to think that our former captives, scattered as they may be, are enjoying a life along ponds and streams not much different from what we observed by our garden pool.

XIX. A FIRST VIEW OF THE TROPICS (BARRO COLORADO 1950)

"Barro Colorado is comfortable. Living conditions at the laboratory so nearly approach the luxurious that one constantly feels in an apologetic frame of mind toward those naturalists who, to reach primeval surroundings, have gone further, fared worse, and seen less. One finds, for example, no descriptions of the abudance of tropical wild life in Nicaragua and Amazonia in the works of Belt, Bates, and Wallace that compare with our almost daily experiences." – Frank M. Chapman.

Any naturalist longs to visit a tropical forest, especially if he happens to have read such books as "My Tropical Air Castle" and "Life in an Air Castle" by Frank M. Chapman. Each offers superb descriptions of Barro Colorado, an island created by the waters of Gatun Lake in the Panama Canal. The story of how the island was made into a sanctuary for the study of wild life and of how the laboratory was built overlooking the lake is told by Chapman. I wondered how one could ever get to such a paradise, when hard-pressed as I was with a wife, young children and a house to pay for in Bethesda, Maryland.

I was favored in this predicament by the remark of a colleague who like myself was a commisssioned officer in the U.S. Public Health Service. He had just gotten a free ride to Texas on MATS (Military Air

Transportation Service). My mind immediately flashed with visions of the jungle. Could I hitch a ride to Panama?

I could try. Jane drove me to Andrews Air Force Base near Washington on an exceedingly cold day in February. I had telephoned ahead to find out if there was a plane headed in the direction of Mobile, Alabama. Yes, I was told; a heavily-crowded hospital plane. My informant said that without priority and without orders my chances of hitch-hiking were next to nil. I could wait at the field if I wished.

How cold it was! I wore the same olive drab uniform I had worn as an officer in the Army Medical Corps in England during World War II. I had put on a major's insignia (the equivalent of my rank in the Health Service) but, as I later found, I had inverted them. Over the uniform I had all the warm clothes I could wear. Little did I expect that I would be sweltering 48 hours later in the mid-July heat and humidity of Panama.

When the hospital plane taxied in and the doors opened, I found it almost empty. No one objected to my riding to Mobile and I was elated to get there. But barriers arose. I had no priority, no orders, no passport; my vaccination was out-dated. How could I leave the country? The lieutenants, warrant officers and sergeants I talked with were sympathetic but equally confused. Then a naval officer, seeing the anchor on my Public Health Service insignia, said, "Oh, I see. You must be in the navy. Yes, there is a plane leaving for Panama tonight."

An empty transport plane landed me the next morning at Albrook Air Base, near Balboa in Panama. I was conspicuous, sweltering in the olive drab uniform. The military personnel on the base were all in light khaki. To my rescue came Dr. James Zetek, the wonderful man to whom I had written about visiting the island. He was in charge of it and, along with Frank Chapman, Tom Barbour and others, a founder of the laboratory. Zetek knew everybody at the air base.

He talked with officials who allowed that although the method I had used to get to Panama was irregular, they would see that I got home safely. That accomplished, my adventure seemed assured.

A naturalist of the old school, used to cutting corners (as I was forced to do), Dr. Zetek took me to a stop in Panama City. I was soon attired in summer clothes and ready to board an old-fashioned train headed for Frijoles on Gatun Lake. I was ferried from there in a cayuco to Barro Colorado.

Aside from discomfitures occasioned by chiggers, the next two weeks were among the greatest in my life. I had the island to myself. What I lacked mostly was the adequate bird guides now available. I had little to go on.

* * * * * * * * * *

My first view of the forest on the island of Barro Colorado had been from the air, as a migrant would see it, following a night flight from Mobile over the Gulf of Mexico. Among the green trees of the jungle flashed the guayacan, with its canopy of bright yellow flowers. What sorts of wild life was I to find under these forest trees?

Barro Colorado seemed as lifeless at noon as woods by the Potomac on a sultry July day. Targets for field glasses were few. Black and Turkey Vultures soared overhead much as in Washington and around the buildings I saw Blue, Plain-colored and Palm Tanagers. There was a loud "oo-eek, oo-eek" as two Smooth-billed Anis—awkward, long-tailed, blackish birds—alighted in a small tree, quite undisturbed by the mid-day sun.

Seedeaters swayed down the longer blades of grass wherever such occured in patches of shade. These birds are attracted to Barro Colorado by its man-made clearing. I was thrilled as a White Hawk, with prominent black marking on wings and tail, circled and screamed at tree-top height. The large buteo seemed out of place with plumage rivaling that of a Snowy Owl or a gyrfalcon.

I left the clearing, glasses at the ready, heading for jungle trails. Huge trees with buttressed roots were draped with lianas and festooned with epiphytes. But not a bird could I find, other than the shadows of omnipresent vultures as they soared above the forest. I began to wonder whether the jungle was deserted or whether I was not sharp enough to pick up the activity that I felt must be surrounding me.

After four days on the island I found that making observations involved strategies that I developed with experience.

The jungle was not dense. Trees were well-spaced and the absence of small plants on the forest floor—coupled with elimination of dead wood by termites—left the ground relatively clear of obstacles. Fallen leaves decomposed so rapidly that they formed no carpet over the bare earth.

The comparative ease of observing mammals was a compensation for lulls in birding. On my first walk I spotted an anteater or tamandua, light brown in color with a jacket of black over its trunk, a short way from the trail. I pushed aside the branches for a closer view and this led him to scramble up a sapling. Climbing for jungle animals is aided by lianas that hang along tree trunks as well as looping from tree to tree.

When I returned to the laboratory I heard ascending "coo" notes coming, I thought, from a tree top. They actually came from a White-tailed Trogon perched bolt upright on a nearby limb. Trogons have bright patterns of blues, greens and yellows. I found a male perched even closer. Both birds, with large placid eyes ringed in white, appeared completely relaxed.

I learned that some jungle birds are surprisingly tame, allowing one to come unexpectedly close. I sometimes had difficulty adjusting my binoculars to the range. On one occasion I looked way up to locate the source of some "caw-caw" notes only to find the bird, a Slaty Antshrike, a mere six feet away.

I suspected that some of these birds spent a good part of each day sitting without making a note. That is why one passed them so easily. North American Warblers though occuring singly and in small numbers, were easy to see due to their activity. I saw Black and White, Chestnut-sided, Yellow, Worm-eating and Prothonotary Warblers while wandering through the forest.

I climbed the long steps to the laboratory buildings as the sun sank behind the trees. Coming to meet me, a step at a time, was an odd creature the size of a small pig. This nine-months-old tapir waved the flexible tip of his nose to find out what manner of individual I was. I was apparently acceptable for he followed me to the porch and rubbed against my chair as I surveyed the prospect over the lake. The tapir reminded me of a small elephant not only by his waving snout but also by his bare hide and pillar-like legs.

Intelligent and companionable, his behavior was unassuming. My only objection was that he had a fondness for untying my shoes. He sniffed me out

along trails where I looked for birds. Sometimes, thinking myself alone as I gazed into the trees, I heard a soft whistle followed by a click. Then a cool nose pressed against my leg as the tapir came to my side.

If I walked up a forest trail he sauntered along behind at his own pace, never interfering with what I was doing. The tapir was my one companion on the island. There were no naturalists or other visitors while I was there. The only residents were a Panamanian and his wife who cooked my meals, cared for the buildings, and generally tended to the island. At that time, alas, I spoke not a word of Spanish.

I was up before dawn each morning, to be out when light first dispelled the night. There were some birds that I could only see in this short in-between period. I sometimes stepped forth when bats, flying in from the forest, were crawling under the edges of the tin roof. A Tropical Screech Owl was often in wait for them. The owl and I then stared at each other from a distance of eight feet before increasing light led it to fly away.

In an area of cleared ground Pauraques or goatsuckers—birds of the night—were still springing into the air after insects.

What mystified me were deep "hoo, hoo" notes coming from the forest . . . notes that I only heard at this time. What kind of a bird could be making them? It was one of the thrills of my stay when I first located a Rufous Motmot. This oddity among birds, perched with bill pointed upward, moved its long, racket-tipped tail in side-to-side swings like the pendulum of a clock. It was a hard bird to find unless it made a sortie after insects.

* * * * * * * * *

Later in the morning, as sun flooded the clearing, I sought out a forest tree with elderberry-like fruit. One of the best strategies for observing birds that I had found was to sit comfortably below such a tree. Then all one had to do was to watch the pageant of life that came before one.

Some of the birds that visited my "elderberry" tree were large and spectacular. Among them were Crested Guans—game birds the size of turkeys that fed on top-most branches. They were quick to take alarm. If I did not sit still, the clamor of their cries implied, in their piteous tone, that I had done a woeful thing in disturbing them. They ran along limbs like squirrels before launching themselves in flight. A glide or clumsy flaps of their wings carried them to neighboring trees.

After the guans had left I settled myself comfortably against a log, rotten enough to yield like a feather bed but strong enough to support a position restful for upward gaze. Thus ensconced, I hoped to remain as motionless as possible. What birds would come next?

Toucans, Swainson's as well as Keel-billed, were the next visitors. They are among the most colorful and grotesque of birds. No matter what a toucan does, it is extraordinary. Just to see one perching with its black plumage offset by brilliant yellow and red markings, and with huge colored bill outlined against the sky, was amazing to me.

The toucans propelled their large bills through the air like boats as they flew into the fruiting tree. Each flapped five or six times before closing its wings completely for a short downward coast and then flapped again. Once arrived, there was something clownish in the way they swung down to reach for berries with the tips of their bills. Berries were propelled to gullets with an upward toss of the head.

Other visitors to the berry tree included a Black-cheeked Woodpecker, a Golden-masked Tanager, a Black-crowned Tityra with its light grey plumage and black wings, and Purple-throated Fruit Crows.

Although I set off following one trail or another on most mornings, there were no obstacles, such as honeysuckle or catbriar, to keep one from wandering into the woods. The jungle was relatively open. Within minutes from a trail I often found myself isolated in a wilderness of tropic vegetation. On some occasions I looked up at the sun-flecked canopies of huge trees and listened to the barks and roars of howler monkeys. Their roars made the jungle seem wonderfully wild and remote.

Sometimes two or three clans of howlers could be heard at a time. But generally they were silent. I often spotted a group in some leafless tree, unmindful of the noonday sun, hunched like so many black porcupines. Their dull black eyes bore a stupid look that reflected little curiosity over my disturbance of the brush below. In passing with comparative slowness from tree to tree howlers anchored their prehensil tails behind, while hanging down to reach for branches with their front limbs.

Capuchin monkeys differed from the howlers. I paused at the foot of a tree one morning to listen to a low "caw" followed by the occasional noise of something dropping through branches. Up above I spotted one, then a number of capuchins in a band extending over many tree tops. Running, leaping and swinging with abandon, they were the epitome of a wild, seemingly carefree existence.

Unlike the dull howler, they came down to peer at me. When I stared back they quickly shifted their gaze, as one seized a small branch or piece of liana with both hands and swung violently to break it off. Now and then screeching accompanied by a display of acrobatics broke out as one capuchin pursued another.

Perhaps the jungle was like this when Balboa first pushed his way through in 1513.

* * * * * * * * * *

Moving slowly along a trail, peering carefully in all directions, I often saw nothing except marvels of the plant world. Scarcely a fly or mosquito disturbed me though I wore no shirt. Yet there were hazards in the jungle: every low leaf and shrub appeared to carry innumerable chiggers awaiting transfer to me as I passed. Every few hours I had to pause for de-infestation. As I sat picking and scratching I felt on a par with the jungle mammals. All of them, from sloth to howler, had the same urge.

I discovered quite by accident a strategy that some-times brought wildlife to view. This was when I had to hurry back to the laboratory one noon to be on time for lunch. The jungle suddenly sprang to life as I swung along the trail with long strides. A sharp "peet" like a passing bullet stopped me short. Close by was a Red-capped Manakin, with crimson head, yellow eyes, black plumage and yellow pantaloons. This wee bird, once found, is readily observed.

As I pounded the trail again I startled a bird from a stump. Sitting placidly before me was a beautiful Violaceous Trogon, showing none of the excitement that one of our northern birds would display on being flushed from its nest. I was able to peer into the partially-covered hollow to see two white eggs resting on fragments of rotten wood. Continuing on I felt I had found another key to the jungle: many tropical birds are so torpid and motionless as to be easily miss-ed unless flushed from their coverts.

Fast movements also seemed, at times, to facilitate seeing mammals. A coatimundi sprang to look at me over the buttressing roots of a huge tree while testing out the breezes with his long, sensitive snout. I often saw only the tail of a coati disappearing in the brush when I moved slowly. Possibly it then had more time to sense my approach.

Wind direction is also important. The ecologist Allee stated that the air is still in the jungle on Barro Colorado. One only needed to blow smoke along a trail, however, to see that breezes were frequent, blowing now this way, now that, because of the ravine-broken contour of the island. One could never tell from which direction a wind might come.

One noon I flushed a collared peccary. It rushed at me, halting within 20 feet. When the proper breeze came along, it fled like a shot.

While striding down a slope on another day I started to step over an obstructing log. Under my foot, and almost as startled as I, was a tayra—a large, black member of the weasel family.

I encountered various kinds of ant birds along the trails, among them the Slaty Antshrike and the Dot-winged Antwren. I wondered whether their black color, prominent in so many jungle animals, had something to do with forest conditions. But some seedeaters, abounding in open places, are as black as the antwrens.

Just before sundown the toucans again set up their noisy chorus. A Swainson's tilted its huge head and bill back to yelp its "dios te de, dios te de te de," joining with others until the jungle resounded. The Keel-billed Toucans uttered a frog-like "quenk, quenk" with endless monotony. I often observed these birds out on the open branches of some tree, leafless in the dry season.

Such trees facilitated other observations. As I stood at dusk one evening, listening to the flute-like notes of a tinamou, my glasses rested on a round termite nest. I was about to pass on when I noted a few sus-picious protuberances.

I rested a bit and looked again. Slowly the ball un-wound and out came the powerful forelimbs and shoulders of a three-toed sloth. The head, when it appeared, was ridiculously small. One needs time to observe the movements of a sloth. The painful slow-ness with which this creature extended a limb re-minded me of an amoeba projecting a pseudopod.

In the course of two days I located three sloths. All resembled immovable termite nests when first found.

A brook flowed under small trees and shrubs by the clearing. Here I occasionally had close view of birds. One day three Yellow-tailed Orioles, all brighter than the Baltimore, bathed in a dark pool. As I climbed up the rocky brook a jet black tanager with white on its wings, appeared in a mass of vines. Then a Long-tailed Hermit, a hummingbird, darted toward me, hovering bolt upright three feet from my face while displaying its long white tail feathers.

The banks of the brook were a good spot for agoutis, sleek brown rodents with heads like short-eared rabbits. They trot about on legs suggestive of those of a miniature horse. I saw several, each with a forefoot raised and hind legs slightly bent in the 'get set' position for a quick escape.

* * * * * * * * * *

When the cayuco took me from the island after two weeks of seeing all kinds of things I had never seen before, I again had a view of the guayacans, each a blaze of yellow flowers. One can hardly appreciate them from the depths of the jungle.

Much as I had seen, there was so much I had not seen. The canopies of high forest trees are a world in themselves. I hoped I could return in later years to become better acquainted with this naturalist's paradise.

On landing at Frijoles railway station, I instantly noticed the greater number of birds and the medley of their notes, as contrasted with the comparatively birdless jungle. Within a short time I saw Blue-black Grasquits, Streaked Saltators, Yellow-green Vireos, Blue Honeycreepers, Grey-breasted Martins, Red-crowned Woodpeckers and others.

Many species of birds seem to thrive where man has disfigured the landscape along the canal. But such changes exterminate guans, toucans and other forest birds. It is fortunate that their jungle habitat is preserved on Barro Colorado.

* * * * * * * * * *

The Panama jungle was the antithesis of what I had seen on an expedition to Northeast Greenland in 1933. The arctic vibrated with life 24 hours a day. Four hours of sleep a night was all one needed in the excitement of watching musk ox, polar bear, phalaropes, jaegers and Dovekies. Everything that ran or flew was visible. The seeming lifelessness of the jungle, in contrast, was at times disconcerting, even though I knew there were unending things to find— if one had the time and experience.

In the arctic summer there is no darkness but most of the 56 or more species of mammals on Barro Colorado, from ocelots to tapirs, are night prowlers. Almost all arctic birds migratory. In the Panama forest only a small proportion migrate and the remainder are a rather sedentary lot. It is said that the tropics have many species, but relatively few individuals; the arctic many individuals but few species.

I was astonished, nonetheless, at the numbers of jungle mammals. If Barro Colorado were suddenly as free of vegetation as the arctic the hundreds of peccaries, agoutis, coatis and monkeys living in a small area would be revealing. The ability of so many birds and mammals to conceal themselves in tropical forests deceives one as to their prevalence. Few visitors see sloths, although they are fairly common.

I have cleared trails through the woods in northern New England and watched with what rapidity the fields turned into forests. The relative openness of the jungle, the ease with which trails can be made and maintained, and the seemingly slow growth of many trees were the reverse of my expectations.

Temperate regions have some characteristics of the tropics, some of the arctic. At different seasons of the year we see Summer Tanagers from one place and Dovekies from the other. One only half knows many of our birds until he has visited those regions north and south where much of their lives are spent.

* * * * * * * * *

When I arrived back at the air base in Panama, I had a surprise. I was told that I had been designated a special courier to carry a locked brief case to the States. A mimeographed sheet detailed the fearsome penalties I was liable to, were I to lose it. What a responsibility after two weeks of carefree life on the island!

The brief case was as heavy as the day was hot. I clung to it tenaciously pouring sweat under my olive drab uniform. I was met by an armed guard when I landed in Mobile. The officer in charge then took the brief case—and, gratefully, not me—into custody!

What a relief!

I had made it to Barro Colorado and returned. I was still covered with chigger bites, but what did they matter compared with my experiences? A love of the tropics had also gotten under my skin, and I had a strong itch to visit them again. This was especially if Jane, less burdened with small children, could come with me.

XX. TWO TROPICAL WOODPECKERS

"He is looking for what he loves . . . Those who are not hunters do not see these things. The hunter is learning to see and to understand . . . to enjoy . . ."–Robert Henri.

One can hunt many kinds of things. Robert Henri was writing of the sketch-hunter and the joy the artist achieves in finding something to enlarge upon later. The amateur philosopher John Locke, who wrote of "hunting and hawking" after ideas, was at another extreme.

To be a naturalist, attempting to work out the behavior of some creature in its natural surroundings, is to combine all of these. There is first the beauty of the bird and the observation of what it does. Then a writing of notes and, importantly, an asking of questions to give one clues of what to seek on succeeding days.

Such activities make one think as well as observe. They combine the good of art, philosophy and much else besides. But I am prejudiced. A naturalist can imagine no more inclusive pursuit than that of natural history. There is nothing more rewarding— especially if he is an amateur and free to do as he likes.

In November of 1970 Jane, our daughter Phoebe and I flew to the Panama Canal Zone where I was to be a visiting virologist at the Middle America Research Unit at Balboa. The lushness of the tropics in the rainy season struck us overwhelmingly from the verandas of Tivoli House where we spent the first night.

Birds were everywhere; Crimson-backed, Blue and Palm Tanagers, orioles, hummingbirds, Scissor-tailed Flycatchers and—out over the Bay of Panama— hundreds of Black Vultures and an occasional Frigate Bird.

What in this wealth of bird life could I find to study effectively, in hours before and after a day at the lab and again on week-ends?

Bird-watching that can be done close at hand is always best. Would opportunities arise?

Within a few days we moved out to a settlement of government houses called Cardenas Village. At first the prospects did not look favorable. But I soon noticed a second growth forest stretching from below our house for half a mile to a cemetery filled with royal palms and flowering trees.

Jane and I were to take many walks in the cemetery. It was a mecca for birds. The inflorescence and fruits of the royal palms drew a steady stream of Blue Dacnis, Orchard Orioles and Clay-colored Robins. The sight of an occasional three-toed sloth in the woods beyond made us feel we would have much to look at in months to come. But what about a discrete problem? How could I find something I really wanted to study; to hunt for day after day, feeling the joy of being on a trail leading somewhere?

"Chance," said Pasteur, "favors the prepared mind." So it seemed on the second morning in the cemetery when I heard a "drr-rr-a" coming from the edge of the forest, a short, obscure sound one would hardly take as the drumming of a woodpecker. Yet I recognized it at once as that of a Crimson-crested, a woodpecker related to the Ivory-billed that drummed in an identical manner.

How could I get through the thick vegetation, close enough for a view? All I got from the outskirts that morning was a glimpse. But later in the day I returned with a machete and hacked at what was to become a network of trails.

The first part of the trail was an immediate success. When the sun rose the next morning, I was already inside the wood when the Crimson-cresteds began drumming. First the male would go "drr-rr-a", then in about 20 seconds, the female would reply. The woodpeckers were relatively tame, not minding my being below. As the first rays of sun flooded under the forest canopy the male flew to his mate's tree and slowly moved toward her as she moved out on a limb. The two then mated not 30 feet from where I stood.

The sight was exciting to me. Here were two birds in the early-morning sun, their flaming red crests and black plumages emphasized by a wide white V on the back and white along the neck. These, I decided, must be the most beautiful of woodpeckers.

Most birds in Panama nest in April or May at the end of the dry season when rains begin. Crimson-crested Woodpeckers are exceptional in getting ready to nest in November when the rainy season is far from over. Here was a marvelous bird to study and to follow wherever it might lead.

I found on succeeding mornings that the wood-peckers came to what I called their "courtship grove." After 20 minutes or so of drumming duets and preening, they flew off in one direction. Was this a

clue to where their nest might be? Could I do enough
hacking with my machete to find out?

It was raining hard a few afternoons later when,
with nothing better to do, I started from the opposite
side of the wood. What a forlorn task, swinging a
machete at one mass of vines after another! The nest
might be anywhere within a square mile. Yet chance
favored me again.

Within five minutes I heard a familiar sound. Incredible! The muffled sounds must be those of a
woodpecker excavating its nest. Moving for a better
view I saw a large stub and at the top, a hole with the
female Crimson-crested looking out.

Returning late in the afternoon, I unfolded my
chair at a distance and sat down to watch. All looked
peaceful in the forest dripping from the recent rain.
Little did I realize how swiftly tragedy can strike.

I heard the woodpeckers approaching and the
female alighted on the stub. She hitched up and
looked in the hole. When her mate alighted below,
she bent down and the two touched bills, a form of
courtship also described for the Ivory-billed. The two
Crimson-cresteds then flew off to feed until the time
of roosting.

As is the custom among woodpeckers, it was the male that returned to the hole and entered, seemingly for the night. He appeared restless, disappearing inside, and then looking out. After ten minutes he emerged.

Then I saw the cause of his nervousness; three Collared Aracaris had arrived. If they looked as piratical to him as they did to me they were a fearsome sight indeed. Aracaris, in addition to being slightly larger and heavier than the woodpeckers, have six-inch bills with black serrations that look like teeth.

There was no contest as to who was to possess the stub. As one Aracari flew to the nest hole, the male Crimson-crested moved away to join his mate at the rear. Both woodpeckers then flew off in the dusk—never to return as far as I was aware.

When I returned to watch by the stub four nights later two Aracaris were sitting side by side watching also. After 20 minutes one, then the other, flew to the hole and entered. How two such ungainly birds could collapse their large bills and snug together in one narrow cavity was difficult to imagine. A third Aracari was left to roost outside.

Although my pair of Crimson-cresteds lost this hole they built another nearer to their courtship grove later on. I was thus able to continue watching while Jane roamed the cemetery enjoying a pageant of tropical bird life that never came to an end.

* * * * * * * * * *

As time passed I extended explorations of the Canal Zone to other patches of forest harboring Crimson-cresteds. One was by the Limbo Hunt Club, a romantic name for a tin roof and cement floor surrounded by an ancient bit of forest. Some trees had huge trunks bearing giant lianas. But as is often the case in the tropics they were surrounded by intervening smaller trees.

The shack was rented by the Middle America Research Unit. One of its members, Dr. Cheniotis, had several natives living there to collect sand flies that rested on the trunks of the giant trees. He had warned me of poisonous snakes. He said his boys had killed a dozen fer-de-lances and three or four bushmasters, the latter being the largest of pit-vipers.

I deplore the killing of snakes, they are so much a part of a forest, but I was prepared to follow Dr. Cheniotis' advice about keeping alert when I arrived one Saturday morning. No one was there. Rain came down in a deluge, making bird watching impossible.

I set out nonetheless along a trail thinking to look for stubs that might harbor nesting woodpeckers, even if I could not see the birds themselves.

The trail was of slippery clay. I swung my machete as I went so that I might find my way back. After a half hour of this slow pace I found a stub with a hole near the top. It appeared deserted and I moved on.

My next pause was at a small opening in the forest, where I gazed at a tree with large dead branches. Perhaps these might have woodpecker holes.

Rain beat on my face, but I figured that if I moved ahead a few steps I could get a better view. It was then that Dr. Cheniotis' warning about watching the trail saved my life. I had taken just one step when I saw something white ahead, standing out against the wet blackness of the forest.

If one can have a cold fright, I had it then. The white was the exposed throat and belly of a six-to-seven foot bushmaster, head raised and ready to strike. One step more and he would have had me, for bushmasters have a long striking range. I hesitated to move at all, then slowly stepped back. The bushmaster lowered its head in the course of a few minutes and moved slowly away.

Feeling that I had had adventure enough for one morning I started back, knowing that if the snake had struck I could never have reached the shack alive.

The snake actually brought me luck. Had I not turned when I did, I would not have arrived at the stub I had noted earlier at the very moment at Crimson-crested Woodpecker flew from the top. A second nest hole!

Once again I was in for disappointment. When I returned some days later I found the stub, heavy and waterlogged from the rains, had crashed to the ground. I was learning something of the hazards of the forest. Toucans had robbed me of one nest and heavy rains of another. Would I ever find one where Jane and I could sit and watch?

* * * * * * * * * *

By January Jane, Phoebe and I were enjoying hours of intermittent sunshine. On Friday afternoons we took the train that runs across the isthmus to Frijoles. There we took a launch across Gatun Lake to the island of Barro Colorado.

Jacanas, a water bird with long toes for running over lily pads, were among birds seen in the crossing.

The landing pier, surrounded by tropical palms, led to a flight of steps to laboratory buildings perched above the lake. The forest was close at hand. Spider monkeys swung out from the trees. Several adult tapirs, large animals weighing hundreds of pounds, came to feed on bread by the kitchen door at dusk.

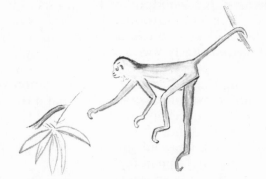

I sometimes paused for a few moments before setting out on one of the trails radiating from the buildings. How should one go about looking for things in such a paradise? It is all too easy to rush off; to try to 'get something done.'

"If you would really see and know a trail," wrote Frank Chapman, "enter it without plan or purpose. Let your motto be where I am is where I'm going. Then you will not be haunted by an objective and, consciously or subconsciously, urged toward it. We are not out for exercise but observation, and are as likely to make it at our doorstep as on the other side of the island. There is apt to run in our head the feeling that the greater the distance the greater the deed. Here, at least, is one place in the world where speed is at a discount. Therefore walk slowly and stop often. Stopping is the very essence of walking."

This is more or less what the three of us did on weekends at Barro Colorado. We wandered over miles of trail, soaked in frequent rains, enjoying many things before we found our first nest of Crimson-cresteds.

Jane discovered it by following a small path near the center of the island. As so often happens in searching for woodpecker nests, the first clue was fresh chips on the ground. The chips lay below a stub 40 feet tall and two feet in diameter. The nest of the Crimson-cresteds was a dark opening, about two-thirds of the way up.

We returned on successive weekends to watch. One might think it tedious to sit on the floor of the forest for hours at a time, but this was not the case. There was an abundance of life as long as the rains continued. We never had to wait long before some creature, a peccary, an agouti, or a coati-mundi came along (the first being a small pig, the second a rabbit-like and the third a raccoon-like animal). All were abundant on the island in the rainy season.

But one had to keep one's eye on the hole in the dark stub in spite of distractions Otherwise one might miss the visits of the woodpeckers.

Sometimes it was only after an hour of waiting that one of the parents flew in to alight. Its mate, out of sight incubating eggs, then swung out. The two birds, especially magnificent when seen together, rested

momentarily side by side before one flew off and the other entered.

These change-overs were silent affairs, the silence reminding one that a tropical forest is full of dangers for nesting birds. The more quietly the woodpeckers came and went the better for their survival.

The forest became increasingly lifeless toward mid-day. A distant thump, thump, thump of a freighter chugging through the lake was often the only sound.

Then abruptly, about four in the afternoon, the jungle came to life. One began to hear noises; deep, throaty howls, increasing in tempo to become a tidal wave of roars crashing through the forest as howler monkeys awakened from mid-day siestas.

These sounds were a thrilling background to watching. One felt that one could wander thousands of miles through the Amazon basin and nowhere see wildlife, especially mammals, as undisturbed or numerous as on the island of Barro Colorado.

* * * * * * * * * *

One morning a band of white-faced capuchin monkeys came along a slanting, vine-grown tree as I sat half-hidden below. They were preceded by a small, bluish hawk that fluttered against the leaves. I soon realized that the hawk was catching insects and other prey frightened by the monkeys.

It is always a thrill to make a discovery. This one reminded me of the way Cattle Egrets catch prey in the grass near moving cattle.

I learned later that I was not the first to note this relation of the Double-toothed Kite to troops of

capuchins. Another ornithologist had written it up a
few years before. But natural history is inexhaustible.
One can always make discoveries that are new in
terms of one's own experience, no matter how much
of what one sees has been recorded by someone else.
The joy of making a discovery is open to those who
will but watch and wait.

* * * * * * * * * *

Some watchers like to spend their time in heroically
long vigils by a nest. While this is important at times, it
can be at the expense of knowing how birds forage
and what types of prey they seek when raising their
young. With this in mind I followed Crimson-crested
Woodpeckers through the forest when opportunities
arose.

One morning I found a male digging grubs from
the top of a well-rotted stub. An adult female, or so I
thought, alighted a foot away. Instead of digging into
the wood as he was doing, she made continuous "k-
da" begging notes. The male suddenly pulled out a
huge grub, as large as one's little finger, then leaned
over and fed it to her. It took some minutes of gag-
ging before she could get it down.

A few minutes later a second female joined the two.
It was a grand sight to see three of these magnificent
woodpeckers together. The second female immediately started to feed herself. I now believed that
the first, or begging female, was a young one of the
year before still following her parents. Had I not
waited to see the whole episode, I might have called it
courtship feeding, something not seen among woodpeckers, common though it may be among other
birds.

I found Crimson-cresteds feeding at other times on
dead limbs under the forest canopy. One might think

it hard to follow them so high up, but they often progressed along the underside of limbs. This was possibly because undersides are moister and more attractive to larvae of insects.

Crimson-cresteds are remarkably agile. By splaying their legs out sideways while directing all four toes outward they can cling to smooth tree trunks or even small branches that might seem precarious for so large a bird.

* * * * * * * * * *

The parent woodpeckers were feeding their young when we returned to watch by the big stub later in January. The male had become cautious as if afraid of something. He spent minutes looking about before approaching his nest. What could be the cause?

At first I wondered whether it might be the Swainson's Toucans, brilliantly-colored birds that came every morning with helping cries to a tree nearby. Did they have designs on his nest hole?

Another possibility was a pair of Spectacled Owls that Jane and I disturbed nearly every time we crept into the thicket where we sat. Or were there other hazards frightening to woodpeckers—perhaps tree-

climbing snakes or tayras (a large form of weasel) that came when we were not there? Something, we knew not what, destroyed the nest the following month.

Another nest gone! A third one had failed! Yet we eventually found a total of seven and, by piecing observations together came to feel that we had gained a fairly inclusive picture of our woodpeckers.

* * * * * * * * * *

It was surprising to find that the Crimson-crested looks much like the Lineated Woodpecker that lives in the same places. Why should two species look so similar?

I had read an article providing an answer before going to Panama. According to the author, the two woodpeckers have similar "ecologies," a situation that would lead to wasteful competition were it not for the woodpeckers being mutually antagonistic and holding territories one against the other. Such interspecific territoriality—for that is what it is called—would be favored by the two species looking alike.

Being no great theorist myself, I was willing to entertain these ideas as a starter. They would give me something to look for. But it took only a few walks along the trails of Barro Colorado to see that the two woodpeckers were not behaving according to theory. Instead of being hostile, they often fed peacefully in the same or in adjacent trees!

Coming slowly up a trail one morning, I heard the "wer, wer, wers" of Lineateds, then the "kwrr-ah" notes of a pair of Crimson-crested Woodpeckers. A male Lineated was working on a limb above, turning and twisting his head to one side, then to the other, while probing a small cavity.

A male Crimson-crested suddenly alighted three feet below. The Lineated moved away a short distance as the slightly larger woodpecker took over. Neither appeared disturbed. The Crimson-crested found nothing of interest, soon moving away a short distance, drumming, and flying off. The Lineated then returned to resume its style of feeding for another 15 minutes. What had been a good feeding place for one had not been for the other.

Man loves to compete but nature moves in the other directions. Competition in feeding or nesting means inefficiency. Where two species such as the Crimson-crested and Lineated overlap, they exploit different resources in different ways.

Crimson-crested Woodpeckers, I found, specialize in knocking bark from dying trees and exposing the larvae of beetles. Lineateds in contrast, feed mainly on ants. This habit attracts them to *Cecropias* that Alexander Skutch calls "most hospitable trees" because they shelter colonies of Azteca ants. Lineateds are able to reach the ants with a few quick blows followed by rapid probings of their flexible tongues.

But why should these woodpeckers resemble each other? My guess is that Crimson-cresteds and Lineateds, despite different habits of feeding and nesting, occupy the same habitat. Both spend their lives moving over trunks and branches in the forest. The problems they face of not being too obvious to predators while remaining visible to others of their own kind are the same for both in the shaded world where they live. Hence, I think, the two species have developed a similar type of plumage by convergent evolution.

* * * * * * * * * *

Following a week-end at Barro Colorado and back again at our home at Cardenas Village, I was sitting on our porch overlooking the patch of second-growth jungle that extended to the cemetery. Sometimes I could find an iguana sunning itself high up in the canopy on a dead branch.

While scanning a tall stub I was electrified to see a whiff of sawdust sparkling in the sun. I called Jane. A Crimson-crested was excavating in view of our house!

After watching for a while I decided to get a closer view, but when I got to the forest edge I found no place to enter. It was an impenetrable wall of vines and thorns. More work for my machete!

Looking more carefully at the excavating wood-pecker I saw to my surprise, when it swung out of the hole, that it was not a Crimson-crested but a Lineated. Here was an opportunity to continue observations begun on Barro Colorado.

Making a trail to the nest was no easy task. I labored for several days, before and after work, getting plenty of exercise. I could see little by craning my neck to look up through the foliage. It became evident that merely getting to the stub would not be enough.

A steep hillside capped by a small cliff lay beyond. I now hacked my way to the top and found I had a fine view of the woodpecker's hole at eye level.

The Lineateds returned each morning to excavate. Sawdust continued to catch the sun's rays as the woodpeckers tossed it from their hole 70 feet above the ground. When the nest was completed, the wood-peckers spent several days resting beside it. Then they disappeared and never returned. Was I left with another enigma?

I continued to watch the stub hoping for some clue as to why the woodpeckers had departed. The stub broke off in a storm a few weeks later at the very place where they had dug their hole.

I wondered whether their excavating might have been part of a strategy. By making holes in high places, relatively safe from predators but precarious in terms of breakage, they may test out places before the time of actual need.

* * * * * * * * * *

In years of enviable birding in Central America, Alexander Skutch appears to have enjoyed woodpeckers especially. His main observations were at roost and nest holes. In one place he speaks of their "happy lives."

His thought has often come to me, perversely, when I have seen nest holes excavated with much toil then lost to Aracaris, to breakage in heavy rains, or to the pillage of some predator, snake or otherwise. One has an impulse to think "how tragic!" Yet I believe the idea that life is tragic rests more in the minds of literary men than in nature.

I have come to envy the lives of Crimson-crested Woodpeckers and other creatures I have watched while sitting for hours in secluded places. These creatures live every day amid scenes of incredible beauty. If natural selection seems cruel at times, it is beneficient in the long run, freeing species from the harassing effects of useless competition. It also shapes each to a special niche in which it can live.

Are these ideas mine or have I heard them elsewhere? Erasmus Darwin, a country doctor in 18th century England, was the one who thought up the idea of evolution by natural selection well ahead of his grandson Charles. It was Erasmus' idea that all creatures delight in life. "The happier they are," he wrote, "the more likely it is that they are well adapted to their environment, and hence will survive."

So I think that Skutch, on the whole, is right about the happiness of woodpeckers. It seems to me that they are happy creatures, inspite of their tragedies, and Jane and I have become the happier for hours spent in watching them.

XXI. OUR AFRICAN HOME

"- - -there is all Africa and her prodigies in us." Sir Thomas Browne.

It was a thrill when I discovered that the British maintained a Virus Research Institute at Entebbe, Uganda, a place that sounded ideal for natural history as well as living. What would be the chance of going there for a year as a visiting scientist? I wrote to the director, Dr. Alexander Haddow and received a kind invitation to come. In our excitement over going, Jane and I read many books on Africa, from "The Man-eaters of Tsavo," to the "Uganda Proctectorate" by Sir Harry Johnson. There is nothing like reading before one travels. It fires the imagination and on arriving, one steps ashore filled with enthuasiasm.

I flew to Africa alone, leaving Jane and our five small children in England to follow a week later. Dr. Haddow met me at the airport that was later to become famous for the "Victory at Entebbe." In those pre-Amin days Uganda was a peaceful and prosperous Eden.

Dr. Haddow was a superactive man of many talents. Yes, he was keen on birds. As I whirled about for several days in his small car he kept pointing them out: "There is *H. senegalensis*; over there *Bycanistes*

subcylindricus, and that one flying is *T. flavirostris.*"
This was real one-up-manship. I could not understand a word he said. How ignorant I felt!

By the time Jane arrived I was established in a low cement house of pleasant proportions. It was surrounded by flowering trees and shrubs, sloping lawns and two avocado trees laden with fruit stood by the kitchen door. The number of birds that came to the garden was fabulous. There was no doubt but that we were to be living in a natural history paradise.

The British that lived about us, all in the Colonial Service, lived by strict codes that seemed to hamstring them from enjoying the beauties of Africa. We were told that it was *de rigueur* to have at least three servants—a cook, a houseboy, and a gardner. I had them hired by the time Jane arrived.

By the end of the first month all of them wanted pay raises. A household with five children, they said, was too much. Each one of them, furthermore, wanted an assistant. They presented a united front to Jane, who was known as "Memsaab" in Swahili.

Jane's answer was simple. They could go. She would do the work herself. The work was really simpler than what she had been doing in Maryland. And so it came about that, with querulous servants gone, our house began to be our own.

I did not feel that it could really become ours unless we had a variety of creatures living with us, so used to this way of life had we become in Bethesda. Africa offered such a wonderful choice of birds, mammals, and reptiles. It seemed a shame, in the time we had, not to become better acquainted with at least some of them.

* * * * * * * * * *

Local Africans soon learned of our interest in animals and began bringing things to us. Most were pathetic specimens arriving in odd parcels—baby sunbirds, doves with broken wings, even a bulbul learning to fly. Only a few were salvageable.

One was a baby ground squirrel with big eyes and a pretty stripe down his side. We called him Nakiwogo. Naki cuddled in a pocket of Jane's apron for some days enjoying the outside world only when being fed milk from a bottle. When weaned, Naki scampered about the living room allowing even the smallest of our totos (Swahili for children) to pull him about.

The Siamese cat eyed Nakiwogo with a hungry expression but was, fortunately, responsive to instruction and refrained from touching any of our pets.

One day a fisherman brought us a four-foot crocodile he had caught in a net. The animal was ferocious at all times when awake. If approached in a friendly manner by someone bringing food, his sides would commence to heave as he worked up the steam of his ferocity. Head and tail would then whip together in a lightning slash.

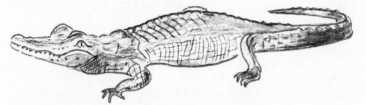

The strategy was obvious. He wanted to knock one of us off our feet and into his mouth, to be snapped between his rows of peg-like teeth. Yet in spite of his ferocity, the crocodile was peaceful when kept among other reptiles and birds that we later acquired.

* * * * * * * * *

Another source of animals was our safaris. One of these was to Ngorongoro Crater in Tanganyika over Christmas time.

When returning I found a large leopard tortoise roaming in semi-desert country well away from the road. It was a heavy load to carry in the hot African sun, but I have always loved turtles. I finally got my prize back to the car.

As we continued through Masailand we came upon a young ostrich separated from its family. Another young one lay on the road, apparently crushed by a truck.

Jane stopped the car as I called to our son Mike, our best animal catcher, to come quickly. The ostrich was fast, but by one of us working one way, the other the other, it had to run close to Mike. Mike dove and caught the bird by the legs.

Where could we put this 3-foot tall bird? Our Ford station wagon, one of the smaller size, was already filled, not only with the seven of us and our gear, but also with horns, skulls, and other prizes Mike had found lying about the bush—not to mention the leopard tortoise.

The ostrich proved a model addition. It sat on the seat with the children as if riding in a car were no new experience. Its long neck was ideal for looking at the passing scene and its eyes, with their long black lashes, had a most human expression.

We drove into Nairobi late in the afternoon. The hotel would have nothing to do with us until we had parked our animals at a local zoo for the night.

The next day we drove through to Eldoret near the Uganda border. The place looked formidable with all of the British, even housewives, carrying tommy guns. We had just driven through Mau-Mau country. Possibly I could take advantage of the disturbance. I said nothing about our pets at the hotel desk, and, when no one was looking, I smuggled them upstairs. Our room had a capacious balcony that the ostrich shared with the tortoise.

The ostrich died by the time we reached Entebbe. This was no surprise to old African hands I have talked to for they have all averred that young ostriches are impossible to raise by hand.

With the addition of his new specimens we now dubbed the wash shed where Mike lived "Mike's Museum". It fairly bulged with horns, tusks, skulls and skins of all manners of animals from antelope and genets to a large otter found dead on the road to Kampala.

A tragedy was that on a later safari we found a magnificent elephant skull. Mike, his brother Peter and I shoved and heaved to get it into the car. But after we had all gotten in, the springs sagged dangerously. We had to abandon our prize.

Mike made additions to his museum in Entebbe as well as elsewhere. Natives brought pythons whenever they speared one in a chicken yard. Starting out at nine feet in length, the skins reached a handsome 12 or more by the time Mike had them nailed onto boards.

* * * * * * * * *

While Mike worked at his museum I had an-Indian carpenter or fundi, a bearded Sikh with a turban, build an outdoor zoo. Our house was formed like a U due to its two wings. It was relatively simple to screen in the space between. One side was formed by our living room, its French window serving as a door by which one could enter.

With the Nile crocodile, the leopard tortoise, a monitor lizard, and my three young hornbills (see next chapter), the zoo made a good start.

Other specimens came to us gradually. One of them was a kite we called Jinja from the town he came from at the outlet of Lake Victoria. Jinja had fallen from his nest as a fledgling.

Kites are scavengers that have adapted to man's ways. We had watched them in downtown Cairo. Dozens of them glided about over Lake Victoria and the Entebbe peninsula on breezy days, their tails tipping from side to side as they balanced in shifting air currents.

Their mewing quavers reminded us more of seagulls than hawks. Also like gulls, the kites swooped for food scraps that our children put out for them on windy days. They fed on the morsels by holding them in both talons while hanging aloft in air currents, for kites can do this as readily as any ordinary hawks perch on a limb.

Jinja took little notice of the other birds although they paid plenty of attention to him. A starling perched on his head and the hornbills liked to preen his feathers. Jinja enjoyed sunbathing—when left alone—and there was never a day without sun at Entebbe. He held his wings with undersurfaces exposed like a man with outstretched arms, palms upward. It was an odd pose that I have never seen in any other bird.

* * * * * * * * * *

One is not apt to think of starlings as being attractive, yet a wealthy lady interested and well versed in aviculture told me that the most endearing bird she had ever had was a hand-raised common Starling. I could believe her readily from our experience with Friendship, a Long-tailed Glossy Starling we raised in Africa.

One day, when driving through central Uganda, I saw a Long-tailed Glossy Starling fly from an old stump. I stopped the car in a cloud of dust and ran to the hole. There were three baby birds inside. With eyes still closed but with pin-feathers well developed they were at a good stage for hand-raising. Their mother darted into the opening with two grasshoppers in her bill when I stood back. She clung to her nest so fearlessly that I had to pick her up to remove one of her young.

The youngster begged for food on the drive home. All we had to offer were insects pulled from the radiator and pieces of sardines left over from lunch. The combination seemed to satisfy and we continued the diet, with variations, for the next week.

By the week's end we were packing for a safari to the Congo. What could we do with our starling? Experience with other pets had taught us that one cannot ask friends to pinch-hit as mother birds. Even the most-well intentioned may not have just the right touch. It was obvious that we would have to take the starling with us.

While Jane and I drove, one of our children kept the fledging happy with pilchards rolled in baby cereal, an exacting task. The bird's appetite was enormous. His eyes were now open and he could see what he ate. It was his incessant friendliness that led us to name him Friendship.

* * * * * * * * *

Once back in Entebbe, we let Friendship have the run of a screened corridor that connected our bedroom with the rest of the house. He developed so well that he was soon rolling peas about the floor and pursuing grasshoppers on his own.

He was joined later by the three baby kingfishers and some honey guides that I kept in small cages prior to sending them to the Smithsonian. Friendship attacked the honey guides whenever he got a chance. But the honey guides, with tough skins evolved to resist bee stings, were impervious to injury. The starling developed a fondness for their special diet of honey mixed with powdered milk and baby cereal.

Friendship flew to us with exuberant cordiality whenever we entered his domain. He was jealous of any attention given to other birds, perching on my shoulder to pinch my ear or pull my hair to let me know of his displeasure. This happened whenever I fed a baby kingfisher or later, other pets. He never did the ear pinching at other times.

One day I arranged sticks in the corridor as perches for the birds. Friendship reacted with harsh screams. He was terrified. He did not react this way to other objects that were new to him and our only explanation was that he may have mistaken them for snakes.

Friendship became increasingly companionable and amusing. He liked to inspect objects of many kinds. If I were reading a magazine, he would perch at the top to see what I found so interesting. If I was writing, he seemed to think that I was wiggling the pen for his benefit. Swift pecks rained on this mysterious dudu (Swahili for insect) that left tracks on paper.

The starling's love of attention was unending. His tail vibrated with pleasure as he cocked his head to look at us when perched on our hands. He sang when we first came to see him in the morning and sometimes just for *joie de vivre*. But he generally preferred to sing when alone.

His attraction to us was so great that it was no easy task to escape from the corridor without his coming along. One had to push him away. This lead him to squeeze under the door but after being caught by the tail several times, he gave up this method of following us. Another strategem was a swoop over our heads into our bedroom. Here he immediately headed for the mirror on the dressing table, finding that other starling reflected in the mirror a very entertaining fellow.

Friendship thus adapted himself to our ways and appeared smart in avoiding hazards such as slamming doors. He was so tame that I let him, one day, hop to the open window. From there he flew to the lawn. I had little doubt that he would come in again, in spite of the world of new things—ants, sticks, and flower petals—that he found to play with.

Then a tragedy that at first seemed irreparable happened. The yard was the territory of three wild Glossy Starlings that had been inspecting a nest hole in a tree above. They alighted by Friendship and attacked. In a flash Friendship was flying for his life with the wild starlings in pursuit. What a pang to see our pet, fleeing into outer space and beyond. Was this the last we would ever see of him?

We called and called without success. It seemed likely that the wild starlings, regarding our garden as their special preserve, would never let Friendship return.

Great was our joy when, toward evening, we spotted Friendship high in a tree. We stood beneath and called, but he seemed to regard us as strangers. Possibly all things in his new outdoor world had an unfamiliar look including ourselves.

Then we thought of his yellow food dish, the one he always used. We filled it with food and set it on the lawn. Friendship flew down at once. It was no trick to get him to hop onto Jane's arm as he ate and we soon had him back in the house. No more of this out-of-door freedom for him. On later occasions, when a door was left open, he showed little interest in crossing the threshold.

* * * * * * * * *

Friendship moved to the outdoor zoo when we had it completed, meeting our three young hornbills, the kite, the leopard tortoise, and others for the first time.

He was not disturbed by these other animals. The hornbills were possibly too grotesque to be recognizable as birds. Friendship would, however, try the ear-pinching trick if I gave them too much attention. I fed the hornbills sliced pawpaw sprinkled with powdered milk. The mixture stuck to my fingers and Friendship was always assiduous in cleaning them for me.

I was a little worried whether the kite, being a hawk, might not seize Friendship one day for a mid-morning snack. He would have liked to, no doubt, for Friendship sometimes pecked him on the head. Yet every night the kite and the starling roosted together on a window ledge in peaceful coexistence.

* * * * * * * * *

There were other animals that I coveted for our zoo but could not acquire. One was a tree hyrax, whose odd cries we had heard nightly in Tanganyika, and another a baby genet. Plain wishing, none the less, seemed to do some good. I wanted a leopard and one day a crate arrived with a five-month-old cub. It was sent us a by a game warden returning to England on leave. Although the leopard was sizeable, we named him Puss Cat.

Calling this name with some trepidation, I reached into the crate and took out an armful of floppy cat with big soft paws. Puss Cat immediately took off on a swift inspection of the house. This brought him face to face with the Siamese cat, who had been sleeping under a bed.

The effect was electric. Never have I seen an animal so terrified. The cat's hair stood on end and his tail was like a bottle brush as he made for the door.

The leopard was now enjoying himself. He leapt about our bedroom, clearing things from chests of drawers and table tops. When I approached, another flying leap brought him straight for my head. I felt his claws and teeth but fortunately only slightly. Puss Cat never drew blood while he was with us.

There were some extra roosters at the Virus Institute and I threw the carcass of a large one to Puss Cat. The leopard pounced, his eyes assuming a fierce expression as he tore off the feathers. We thought it best to leave him alone with his prey, for he was now unmanageable.

It was some minutes before I returned. Puss Cat had pushed a door open and was leaping about our bedroom again, this time shaking and tearing the rooster as he went. It was too dramatic to miss. I hastened back with flash bulbs to record the orgy before we started to pick up the feathers.

That night, knowing what a leopard on the loose could do, I made certain that the doors to the screened corridor were closed. We did not want the leopard landing on us in the dark.

I heard screams at mid-night and leapt from bed. The door at the far end was open. Joshua, aged four, slept in the room beyond. He always slept with the light on and this was just as well. When I reached his room, Josh was at one end of his bed with covers pulled over his head. He kept lifting a corner and then, seeing the leopard, letting out a scream. Puss Cat obviously found this game entertaining, probably more so than spending the night in the corridor. In spite of the screaming he had done no harm.

The next morning Joshua told of a wild animal that had leapt on his bed in the night. When asked the name of the creature in kindergarten, he could not remember. Thus no one believed him and his story fell flat.

The leopard became more docile as time went by. Mike liked to put him on a leash and take him for walks around the garden.

We had read that leopards were fond of dogs and I often wished that we could substitute some of our neighbor's for the roosters in Puss Cat's diet. One of these brutes had been encouraged to bite Africans. This not only had a dampening effect on interracial relations but also encouraged the watchman to linger in a dark corner of the institute garage when he should have been making his rounds at night.

Puss Cat looked competent to deal with a dog of any size. He would sit on his haunches and curl his lips in a ferocious, hungry snarl when one came in sight. We felt constrained, however, to keep the leopard on a rooster diet rather than slip his leash.

The man who had raised the leopard finally came to recover his pet. Puss Cat sprang at his head in a boisterous greeting that left claw marks dripping with blood. He had never hurt any of us—not even the Siamese cat. After he had left, we felt that he had been by far the most beautiful creature we had ever possessed.

* * * * * * * * * *

A month after the Africans had been dismissed by Memsaab, Johanna, the cook, came to the door to say that he liked the children and wanted to work for us again. Johanna came from the Congo and lived more or less isolated among the natives of Uganda. He was a pleasant fellow and, moving about the house in his white, nightgown-like costume and bare feet, became indispensible to us in many ways.

Johanna often came to the living room after supper dishes had been put away. Here I had assembled a collection of native drums. Taking one between his knees and with others within reach, Johanna made our house resound to the music of the Congo. The children as well as ourselves were enthralled.

Johanna was well established when he suddenly disappeared, leaving no word. Had he gone back to the Congo? Six weeks went by and we gave him up for lost. Then, to our astonishment, he came limping into the yard.

Jane and I could not speak Swahili. We had to get an interpreter. The accident that had befallen Johanna, it turned out, was somewhat my own fault.

Africans, as narrated earlier, had been bringing us snakes, already killed, for Mike to skin for his museum. One day the director of the Botanical Garden drove in with a snake his boys had found for us. Other specimens he had brought had all been dead. After the Scotchman had left I opened the box. It was something of a shock to find a live cobra inside.

I got my camera, as well as my panga (machete) and opened the box on the wide lawn. The cobra slithered out, semi-coiled, and spread its hood. I took a series of pictures.

I had little choice about the final disposal of the cobra. I did not want it alive in the garden with our five children. As the snake moved toward the bushes, I killed it with the panga.

It was the next morning that Johanna disappeared. According to his account he had returned to his shamba (native hut) the evening before when he saw a snake slithering by his doorway. Following my example, he reached for his panga, but the snake struck first.

A hospital was fortunately nearby, otherwise Johanna might not have lived. As it was he had a most uncomfortable time.

It was good to have Johanna back with us again. With the hornbills, Friendship the starling, the leopard, the leopard tortoise and others, plus Mike's museum and the drums with Johanna playing them, our African home was again in full swing. We felt, as Sir Thomas Browne expressed it that there was "all Africa and her prodigies in us."

XXII. THE AFFECTIONATE
HORNBILLS

"The hot-springs of love run deep and pervasive in the clay of all vertebrates. It is not surprising that their external bubblings appear to be much the same in a university graduate, an Australian bushman, or a lowly sparrow."
J. C. Welty.

Most birds have pair bonds that last only through a nesting season. Others, particularly in the tropics, may be mated the year round or even for life. But no birds take their pair bonds for granted. They have small rituals, ceremonies and mannerisms of expressing affection for each other many times a day.

This seemed especially true of a pair of Black and White Casqued Hornbills that roosted in a tree outside our bedroom window in Entebbe.

Jane and I often sat in the garden to watch them. They would sail in with fair regularity shortly before seven o'clock, then snuggle together for a while before separating to their individual roosts. Their roosting perches, the same every night, were about 20 feet apart, possibly for safety from predators.

Soon after coming in, the male would give a heave and a small fruit would pop from his gullet to his bill tip. His mate would refuse the offering. Then he would send the fruit flying back to his gullet with a backward toss of his head, only to try the performance again a few minutes later. She might refuse four times in a row without discouraging him. In fact, she almost never accepted.

Female hornbills have the unusual habit of cementing themselves inside a hollow tree during nesting season. The male had shown, if only by ceremony, his readiness to feed her at a later date when she was walled in her nest.

Another demonstration of affection after the attempted courtship feeding was that of preening each other's head feathers. The male nibbled small feathers under his mate's bill as her head went farther and farther back until her throat was fully exposed. In this grotesque position her head feathers would ruffle up in ecstatic contentment. After a time she reciprocated by nibbling at the base of feathers on his head—with an expression of devotion that continued until the two separated at dusk.

We kept track of our hornbills during the night by their various odd woofs and bill-wackings that increased toward dawn. When the Woodland Kingfisher gave his first song and the bulbuls called "quick, doctor, quick" the hornbills again snuggled together against the cool morning air. Only at sunup did they fly away with an outburst of calls and lamentations.

* * * * * * * * * *

Most of my hornbill-watching was carried on at Mpanga rather than in our garden. This patch of forest, with a network of trails cut by the forestry department, was virtually a last refuge for hornbills. Remnants of forest elsewhere were disappearing to make room for more Buganda, with their bicycles and bananas.

On my first visit to Mpanga the forest seemed desolate until I came to an unusually large and beautiful tree that grew by a crossing of two trails. Six feet through at its base, the trunk of smooth bark rose 70 feet or more before dividing into huge limbs, most of them overgrown with cabbage ferns and other epiphytes. These supported lianas that dropped to the forest floor.

A male hornbill was perching above a broken stub on a large limb. His mate was in a cavity below, walled in with cement excepting for a slit one to two inches wide and eight inches long, through which I could see the tip of her beak moving about inside. The male was an odd-looking creature over two feet long, with a huge beak made even more impressive by a forward-projecting casque.

On returning to the headquarters clearing I discovered a second pair of hornbills cementing their nest hole. Here was a good nest to study and I watched construction over subsequent week-ends. The female would remain inside the hole for an entire morning while her mate perched just outside. I could hear her bill tapping the cement into place as she proceeded with infinite care.

The male's job was that of a bricklayer's helper. Every so often he gave a heave and popped a pellet from his gullet to his bill tip. He then bent down to present it to his mate. She continued her plastering, taking as many as ten pellets one after another. They were so engrossed in their work that they made little noise.

The male beat his way to the forest clearing from time to time to swoop down among the native huts. I was keen to learn what he picked up. On one occasion he landed behind the forest ranger's house. Using this as cover I ran up, then worked my way around to a patch of corn. From this hiding place I saw the male on a low stump 30 feet away. Mid-morning sun brought out a bluish tinge to his black feathers, as his huge head swung down to pick up and swallow chunks of earth. His mate in the meantime had left the nest to perch by the clearing. He flew up and fed her eleven pellets, which she swallowed before flying over to a paw-paw tree. I believed she needed the fruit juices to soften the dry earth he had given her.

I went over to look at the stump. The male had torn open a termite's nest. I could see soldiers rushing out to stand guard and workers swarming to rebuild the broken tunnels. Here was a discovery!

These hornbills, as I learned on subsequent occasions, use termite earth for their cement, just as some Africans use it to make floors for their huts. Termites, in building their mounds, coat each grain of earth with glue. This material becomes as hard as rock on drying.

Some weeks later I spent the night in a native hut at the edge of the forest. At dawn I walked down the cool, damp forest trail leading to the giant *Toxicaria* where I had found the first nest. As I did so I frightened the male, who flew away with a terrible noise—as though all his gears were unoiled and grinding. Other hornbills were flying back and forth to fruiting trees, their calls rising in a crescendo. All this was augmented by the screamings of parrots and plantain-eaters.

Fifteen minutes later the male returned to the nest. He perched above the entrance to cough up four yellow fruits that he placed one by one in the tip of his mate's bill. Then he flew to another tree to whack his beak in resounding fashion. His mate meanwhile rattled her bill in the entrance, screaming loudly. Possibly he had not brought her enough breakfast.

The view from her home in the limb must have been a magnificent one over the tops of the jungle trees. Her mate enlivened her long vigils by returning every 30 to 50 minutes with more fruit.

* * * * * * * * * *

One morning I heard a commotion among both Casqued and Pied Hornbills. The center of their alarm was a magnificent hawk-eagle perched just below the forest canopy.

When it had flown away I found myself in a new area of the forest. I listened intently for other birds that might be there. Then I heard some tapping. Walking carefully along a trail I discovered a hornbill nest only 30 feet from the ground. All other nests had been located about 80 feet up, well beyond hope of reaching them. But this one was a possibility!

Fetching the African forest ranger, I showed him that we could climb to the nest by tying ladders together and using poles for a scaffold. Everything was in place by the following week-end. I climbed the swaying ladders with flashlight in hand to look in. To my surprise there were two white eggs but no mother bird. I pointed the flashlight around at all angles and finally found that she had an escape chamber directly above her nest. Only the tip of her tail was in sight.

On the following Saturday the ranger told me that two eggs had been there earlier that morning. On approaching I scrutinized the forest floor. An eggshell with ants swarming over its moist membrane lay below the entrance. I climbed to the nest. Inside was a tiny, blue-skinned chick. This was my first view of Mpanga, who was to live with us later, first in Africa and then in America for nearly three years.

The second egg hatched four days later. This chick lived for only a week, doubtless dwarfed from the start by its brother. It seemed that hornbills lay two eggs in case one should fail to hatch. If all young were raised there would not be room enough in a nest.

* * * * * * * * * *

I eventually found a total of 16 hornbill nests, many too inaccessible for steady watching. One was fortunately located in the Entebbe Botanical Garden in a long, arching limb of a *Piptadenia*. The tree stood below a hill overlooking the lake and was ideally situated for making observations.

One November afternoon I sat on the hill looking into the cavity at almost eye level. With the sun behind me I could see the female tapping with her bill from the inside. Her mate, whom I called Winnie, flew in my direction several times on his way to gather earth from a termite mound.

Activities of the pair changed a few evenings later. Winnie now hopped about the tree in restless fashion before flying off to return with some fruit. Then he bent over the hole to feed his mate.

By the last rays of the sun I could see that the wall was now complete. Dusk had come as Winnie finally flew over the hill with a whooshing of wings. This was the evening when the female began her long period of voluntary imprisonment. The two hornbills, until now virtually inseparable, would not be together again for four months. They would see each other only for brief moments when the male came for a feeding visit.

Winnie had flown away, rather dramatically, to the sound of taps from the police barracks and the rising of a full moon.

* * * * * * * * * *

The Botanical Garden was pleasantly fresh and cool before breakfast. Africans walked to work as the sun came up, some of them nonchalantly swinging their hands as they balanced lawn mowers on their heads. I liked to stand by a flowering bush, from whence I got the best view of the hornbill's nest.

Flocks of parrots with short, rapid wing-beats accompanied by mingled whistles and screams conducted regular flights from islands in the lake. Sometimes I had to wait 15 or 20 minutes for the sound of Winnie's approach. He was always spectacular: the early sun shone on his black-and-white plumage and huge casque as he crossed a stretch of lawn.

One morning he brought more than breakfast for his mate. With head held high, his bill clamped on a short stick that projected to one side so much like a cigar that I was reminded of Sir Winston Churchill. Winnie alighted on the arching limb of the *Piptadenia,* then bounced sideways until he rested belly flat above the nest. His head swung down to offer the stick. No food came until it was accepted. Winnie then coughed several times, popped a fruit from his gullet and presented it to his mate, who then took six more in succession. He gave a chuckle each time his head swung down. Winnie bounced to another perch after the feeding to whack his bill against the bark before flying off with the familiar whooshing of wings.

I never tired of seeing Winnie fly to the nest during my four months of pre-breakfast visits to the Botanical Garden. But on an increasing number of them I noticed that he was no longer alone. An odd female, whom I called Clytemnestra, followed Winnie with growing frequency to the *Piptadenia.*

Who this lady was I never learned. I began to wonder whether seduction was possible among hornbills. Winnie was a carefree bachelor excepting for brief intervals during the day. It was easy to provide food where fruiting trees were abundant. Clytemnestra might well edge in on his leisure time.

One morning Winnie seemed in doubt. He fed his mate, then bounced and hopped upward to where the odd female was waiting. Winnie knocked off a piece of bark.

In the hornbill's world, presentation of a piece of bark or a stick is a token of affection. Winnie clamped on the bark a number of times until it was nearly broken up. Then he moved closer to the intruder. Would he present what remained to Clytemnestra?

To my relief he flew back to his big limb, bounced over to the hole and, swinging his casqued head down, presented the remnants to his mate.

I came to feel—at this moment, and at others—that paired hornbills have a tremendous attachment to each other, otherwise their long nesting ordeal could never succeed. Yet, on the other hand, a hornbill without a mate must feel especially miserable.

Possibly this explained Clytemnestra's persistent pursuit of Winnie. Sometimes he would interrupt his feeding to chase her away. But her persistence was unshaken. When Winnie flew from the *Piptadenia* she would tag along 20 feet behind.

In early March I visited the garden to find Clytemnestra more of a devil than I had supposed. She had come to the nest alone and was knocking pieces from the cement wall, then crumbling them in her bill. I waited in suspense. After some minutes a whoosh of wings announced Winnie's approach. Only then did his own mate, silent when under attack, give way to screams of alarm from within her hollow limb.

Her long siege was nearly over. Five days later, four months from the evening Winnie had first flown over the hill alone, mother and young emerged. This was after knocking away the entrance wall that fell to the ground as a solid piece of cement. Hearing hornbill noises toward the lake, I went over to find Winnie and his mate snuggled together as before the nesting ordeal.

His head went back as she nibbled at the feathers on his throat. Her plumage was soiled. The feathers on the top of her head were worn from long confinement in cramped quarters. But this made no difference to Winnie. His head went back still further in the enjoyment of having those inaccessible feathers in his throat nibbled and preened once more.

The idyll was spoiled by only one circumstance: Clytemnestra was perching just a few trees away.

I could not find the young hornbill at this time. But the following morning a chance bird-watcher saw a female hornbill (Clytemnestra?) attacking it savagely. I later found it clinging to a tree near its parents. It appeared to be crippled. I picked it up when it fell to the ground. Its foot was broken. Knowing that it might become a victim of the next passing dog or cat, I carried the young male hornbill to the car—despite Winnie's swooping at my head repeatedly.

Jane and I named the young hornbill Mpigi as we bound his foot in a metal splint. Mpigi spent his first

days on the ground in the outdoor zoo of our Entebbe home. Within a week he was able to leave his
lowly associates—the leopard tortoise and Nile
crocodile—and perch with our other two young
hornbills. By April he was completely cured.

I went back to the Botanical Garden on the afternoon of Mpigi's capture. His parents were back by
their nest tree and, as I was turning to leave, I heard a
flutter of wings. Looking back, I saw both Winnie and
his mate hard in pursuit of Clytemnestra.

This was the last I saw of this evil genius. Whether
she was an offspring from a former year who felt
rejected, or just a lone female who recognized Winnie
as something special, I shall never know.

* * * * * * * * *

I believed that I had seen the last of Winnie and his
mate, but such was not the case. Various hornbills
passed through our garden. One pair came to stay
and perched much of the time in trees close to the
outdoor zoo. Their cuks and wailings resounded
throughout the house. The male would occasionally
swoop down over the wire netting that held our captives.

Curiosity aroused, I compared his bill markings
with sketches in my notebrook: there was no doubt as
to his identity. Winnie and his mate had found their
lost young one! They had come to us from the Botanical Garden two miles away. For the next six weeks
until we left Entebbe, they spent much of each day in
our garden, making an almost continual commotion.
Such was their devotion to their young one.

* * * * * * * * *

The only opening into the large cage containing the hornbills was the living-room window. When I opened it at breakfast time Friendship was the first to greet us. After we had sat down to breakfast, the three hornbills Mpanga, Zika and Mpigi whooshed through the dining room to perch on the edge of the table for their usual bits of toast dipped in coffee.

Once in a while they dropped in for other meals, hopping over the table to inspect all plates but never neglecting the flower centerpiece. Appetites satisfied, they whooshed back through the living room and out to their cage. There might be a few odd droppings to clean up on the cement floor, but nothing more.

It was wonderful to have hornbills living close at hand, where I could continue studies on their behavior. Jane was patient most of the time. But occasionally it was too much. She would then get up with Friendship in her hair and a hornbill on each arm to take them to their cage. The house then became free, at least momentarily, from the din and commotion of an African jungle.

BIBLIOGRAPHY

Bent, A. C. Life histories of North American cuckoos, goatsuckers, hummingbirds and their allies, *U.S. Nat. Mus. Bull.*, 176, 1940

Beston, Henry, *The Outermost House*, New York, 1933

Cahalane, Victor H., *Mammals of North America*, New York, 1947

Chapman, Frank M., *My Tropical Air Castle*, New York-London, 1929

Chapman, Frank M., *Life in an Air Castle*, New York-London, 1938

Cochran, Doris, M., and Goin, Colman, J., *The New Field Book of Reptiles and Amphibians*, New York, 1970

Cornwell, G. W., Observations on the breeding biology and behavior of a nesting population of Belted Kingfishers, *Condor* Vol. 65, 426-431, 1963

Huxley, Julian S., The courtship-habits of the Great Crested Grebe (*Podiceps cristatus*), with an addition to the theory of sexual selection, *Proc. Zool. Soc. Lond.*, 491-562, 1914

Johnston, Sir Harry, *The Uganda Proctectorate*, London, 1902

Kauffeld, Carl, *Snakes and Snake Hunting*, New York, 1957

Kilham, Lawrence, Courtship behavior of the Pied-billed Grebe, *Wilson Bull.* Vol. 66, 65, 1954

_____, Repeated territorial attacks of Pied-billed Grebe on Ring-necked Duck, *Wilson Bull.*, Vol. 66, 265, 1954

_____, Breeding and other habits of Casqued Hornbills (*Bycanistes subcylindricus*), *Smithsonian Miscell. Coll.*, Vol. 131, 1-45, 1956

_____, Head-scratching and wing-stretching of woodpeckers, *Auk*, Vol. 76, 527-528, 1959

_____, Breeding behavior of Yellow-bellied Sapsuckers, *Auk*, Vol. 79, 31-43, 1962

_____, The relations of breeding Yellow-bellied Sapsuckers to wounded birches and other trees, *Auk*, Vol. 81, 520-527, 1964

_____, Differences in feeding behavior of male and female Hairy Woodpeckers, *Wilson Bull.*, Vol. 77, 134-145, 1965

_____, Reproductive behavior of Yellow-bellied Sapsuckers. I. Preference for nesting in *Fomes* infected aspens and nest hole interrleations with flying squirrels, raccoons, and other animals, *Wilson Bull.*, Vol. 83, 159-171, 1971

_____, Caterwauling of the Barred Owl: A speculation, *N.H. Aud. Quart.* Vol. 25, 93-94, 1972

_____, Habits of Crimson-crested Woodpeckers in Panama, *Wilson Bull.,* Vol. 84, 28-47, 1972

_____, Interspecific actions of sexual signals among hand-raised woodpeckers, *Avic. Mag.,* Vol. 80, 104-108, 1974

_____, Play in Hairy, Downing, and other Woodpeckers, *Wilson Bull.,* Vol. 86, 35-42, 1974

_____, Biology of young Belted Kingfishers, *Am. Mid. Nat.,* Vol. 92, 245-247, 1974

_____, Winter foraging and associated behavior of Pileated Woodpeckers in Georgia and Florida, *Auk,* Vol. 96, 15-24, 1976

Lorenz, Konrad Z., The Companion in the birds world, *Auk,* Vol. 54, 245-273 1937

_____, *King Solomon's Ring,* New York, 1952

Patterson, J. H., *The Man-eaters of Tsavo,* London, 1952

Peterson, Roger Tory, A Field Guide to the Birds, Boston, 1947

Skutch, Alexander F., *Life histories of Central American Birds III,* Pac. Coast Avif. No. 35, Berkeley, 1969

LIST OF SPECIES

The species mentioned in this volume are listed below alphabetically by vernacular names, each followed by the scientific name.

Agouti, *Dasyprocta aguiti*
Alligator, *Alligator mississippiensis*
Angel Wing, *Cyrtopleura costata*
Anhinga, *Anhinga anhinga leucogaster*
Anole, *Anolis carolinensis*

Badger, *Taxidea taxus*
Baltimore Oriole, *Icterus galbula*
Banded Water Snake, *Natrix fasciata*
Barred Owl, *Strix varia*
Bay-breasted Warbler, *Dendroica castanea*
Bear, *Ursus americanus*
Beaver, *Castor canadensis*
Belted Kingfisher, *Megaceryle alcyon*
Black-bellied Plover, *Squatarola squatarola*
Black-cheeked Woodpecker, *Centurus pucherani*
Black-crowned Tityra, *Tityra inquisitor*
Black Duck, *Anas rubripes*
Black-poll Warbler, *Dendroica striata*
Black Skimmer, *Rynchops nigra nigra*
Black Snake, *Coluber constrictor*
Black-throated Blue Warbler, *Dendroica caerulescens*
Black Vulture, *Coragyps atratus*
Black and White Casqued Hornbill, *Bycanistis subcylindricus*
Black and White Warbler, *Mniotilta varia*
Bluebird, *Sialia sialis*
Blue-black Grasquit, *Volitinia facarina*
Blue Dacnis, *Dacnis cyana*
Blue Honeycreeper, *Cyanerpes cyaneus*
Blue Tanager, *Thraupis cana*
Blue-winged Teal, *Anas discors*
Boat-tailed Grackle, *Cassidix mexicanus*
Bobcat, *Lynx rufus*
Brown-headed Nuthatch, *Sitta pusilla*
Brown Pelican, *Pelecanus occidentalis carolinensis*
Bulbul, *Pyncnotus tricolor*
Bufflehead, *Bucephala albeola*
Bull Frog, *Rana catesbiana*
Bushmaster, *Lachesis mutus*

Calico Scallop, *Aequipecten gibbus*
Canada Goose, *Branta canadensis*
Canebrake Rattlesnake, *Crotalus horridus atricaudatus*
Cape May Warbler, *Dendroica tigrina*
Capuchin, *Cebus capucinus*
Cardinal, *Richmondena cardinalis*
Carolina Wren, *Thyrothorus ludovicianus*
Cattle Egret, *Bubulcus ibis*
Chamois, *Rupicapra rupicapra*
Channeled Whelk, *Busycon canaliculatum*
Chestnut-sided Warbler, *Dendroica pensylvanica*
Chickadee, *Parus atricapillus*
Chigger, *Sarcopsylla penetrans*
Chipmunk, *Tamias striatus*
Chuck-will's-widow, *Caprimulgus carolinensis*
Clapper Rail, *Rallus longirostris*
Clay-colored Robin, *Turdus grayi*
Coatimundis, *Nasua nasua solitaria*
Collared Araceri, *Pteroglossus torquatus*
Collared Peccary, *Tayassu tajacu*
Common Atlantic Slipper, *Crepidula fornicata*
Common Crow, *Corvus brachyrhynchos*
Common Gallinule, *Gallinula chloropus*
Coot, *Fulica americana*
Cormorant, *Phalacrocorax auritus*
Cottonmouth, *Agkistrodon piscivorous*
Crested Flycatcher, *Myiarchus crinitus*
Crested Guan, *Penelope purpurascens*
Crimson-backed Tanager, *Ramphocelus dimidiatus*
Crimson-crested Woodpecker, *Campephilus melanoleucos*
Crocodile, *Crocodylus niloticus*

Deer, *Odocoileus virginianus*
Diamondback Rattlesnake, *Crotalus adamanteus*
Diamondback Terrapin, *Malaclemys terrapin*
Dolphin, *Tursiops truncatus*
Dot-winged Antwren, *Microhopias quixensis*
Double-toothed Barbet, *Lybius bidentatus*
Double-toothed Kite, *Harpagus bidentatus*
Dovekie, *Plantus alle*
Downy Woodpecker, *Picoides pubescens*
Dunlin, *Erolia alpina pacifica*

Eider, *Somateria mollissima*
European Kingfisher, *Alcedo attis*

Fer-De-Lance, *Lachesis lanceolatus*
Ferret, *Mustela putorius*
Fish Crow, *Corvus ossifragus*
Fisher, *Martes pennanti*
Flicker, *Colaptes auratus*
Flying Squirrel, *Glaucomys volans*
Fox, *Vulpes fulva*
Frigatebird, *Fregata magnificens*

Gadwall, *Anas strepera*
Garter Snake, *Thamnophis sirtalis*
Genet, *Genetta genetta*
Giant Atlantic Cockle, *Dinocardium robustum*
Golden-crowned Kinglet, *Regulus satrapa*
Golden-masked Tanager, *Tanagra larvata*
Grackle, *Quiscalus quiscula*
Great Blue Heron, *Ardea herodias*
Great Crested Grebe, *Podiceps cristatus*
Great Egret, *Casmerodius albus egretta*
Great Horned Owl, *Bubo virginianus*
Green Heron, *Butorides virescens*
Grey-breasted Martin, *Progne chalybea*
Grey Fox, *Urocyon cinereoargenteus*
Grey Squirrel, *Scicurus carolinensis*
Grey Woodpecker, *Mesopicus goertae*
Gull, *Larus argentatus*

Hairytail Mole, *Parascalops breweri*
Hawk-Eagle, *Stephanoaetus coronatus*
Hermit Thrush, *Hylocichla guttata*
Honey Guide, *Indicator indicator*
Hooded Merganser, *Lophodytes cucullatus*
Hoopoe, *Upupa epops*
House Sparrow, *Passer domesticus*
Howler Monkey, *Alouatta palliata*
Huia, *Heteralocha acutirostris*
Hummingbird, *Archilochus colubris*

Iguana, *Iguana tuberculata*

Jacana, *Jacana hypomelaena*

Keel-billed Toucan, *Ramphastos sulfuratus*
Kingbird, *Tyrannus tyrannus*
King Snake, *Lampropeltis getulus*
Kite, *Elaneus caeruleus*

Least Shrew, *Cryptotis parva*
Leopard, *Panthera pardus*
Leopard Tortoise, *Testudo pardalis*
Lesser Scaup, *Aythya affinis*
Lineated Woodpecker, *Dryocopus lineatus*
Loggerhead Turtle, *Caretta caretta*
Long-tailed Glossy Starling, *Lamprotornis caudatus*
Long-tailed Hermit, *Phaethornus superciliosus*
Loon, *Gavia immer*
Louisiana Heron, *Hydranassa tricolor ruficollis*

Malachite Kingfisher, *Corythornis cristata*
Marbled Godwit, *Limosa fedoa*
Marsh Hawk, *Circus cyaneus hudsonius*
Martin, *Martes americana*
Meadow Mouse, *Microtus pennsylvanicus*
Mink, *Mustela vison*
Mockingbird, *Mimus polyglottos polyglottos*
Mole Snake, *Lampropeltis calligaster rhombomaculata*
Monarch butterfly, *Dancus plexippus*
Monitor Lizard, *Varanus niloticus*
Mourning Dove, *Zenaidura macroura*
Mud Turtle, *Kinosternon subrubrum*
Muskrat, *Ondatra zibethica*

Newt, *Notophthalmus viridescens*
Northern Shrike, *Lanius excubitor*

Ocelot, *Felis pardalis*
Osprey, *Pandion haliaetus carolinensis*
Ostrich, *Struthio camelus*
Otter, *Lutra canadensis*
Orchard Oriole, *Icterus spurius*

Painted Bunting, *Passerina ciris*
Palm Tanager, *Thraupis palmarum*

Parula Warbler, *Parula americana*
Pauraque, *Nyctidromus albicollis*
Philadelphia Vireo, *Vireo philadelphicus*
Pied-billed Grebe, *Podilymbus podiceps*
Pied Crow, *Corvus albus*
Pied Hornbill, *Tockus fasciatus*
Pied Kingfisher, *Ceryle rudis*
Pileated Woodpecker, *Dryocopus pileatus*
Pine Grosbeak, *Pinicola enucleator*
Pine Siskins, *Spinus pinus*
Pine Warbler, *Dendroica pinus*
Pintail, *Anas acuta tzitzihoa*
Piping Plover, *Charadrius melodus*
Plain-colored Tanager, *Tangara inornata*
Porcupine, *Erethizon dorsatum*
Prairie Warbler, *Dendroica discolor*
Prothonotary Warbler, *Protonotaria citrea*
Purple-throated Fruit Crow, *Querula purpurata*
Pygmy Kingfisher, *Ispidina picta*

Raccoon, *Procyon lotor*
Rat Snake, *Elaphe obsoleta*
Redback Mouse, *Clethrionomys gapperi*
Bed-bellied Water Snake, *Natrix erythrogaster*
Red-bellied Woodpecker, *Centurus carolinus*
Red-breasted Nuthatch, *Sitta canadensis*
Red-capped Manakin, *Pipra mentalis*
Red-cockaded Woodpecker, *Picoides borealis*
Red-crowned Woodpecker, *Centurus rubricapillus*
Red Crossbill, *Loxia curvirostra*
Red-headed Woodpecker, *Melanerpes erythrocephalus*
Red-shouldered Hawk, *Buteo lineatus*
Red Squirrel, *Tamiasciurus hudsonicus*
Red-tailed Hawk, *Buteo jamaicensis*
Ring-billed Gull, *Larus delawarensis*
Ringed Kingfisher, *Ceryle torquata*
Ring-necked Duck, *Aythya collaris*
Ringneck Snake, *Diadophis punctatus*
Royal Tern, *Thalasseus maximus*
Ruddy Turnstone, *Arenaria interpres*
Ruffed Grouse, *Bonasa umbellus*
Rufous Motmot, *Urospatha martii*

Sanderling, *Crocethia alba*
Scaup, *Aythya marila nearctica*
Scissor-tailed Flycatcher, *Muscivora forficata*
Seal, *Phoca vitulina*
Seedeater, *Sporophila aurita*
Shorttail Shrew, *Blarina brevicauda*
Skunk, *Mephitis mephitis*
Slaty Antshrike, *Thamnophilus punctatus*
Smooth-billed Ani, *Crotophaga sulcirostris*
Snapping Turtle, *Chelydra serpentina*
Snowshoe Hare, *Lepus americanus*
Snowy Egret, *Leucophoyx thula*
Solitary Sandpiper, *Tringa solitaria*
Sora, *Porzana carolina*
Spectacled Owl, *Pulsatrix perspicillata*
Spider Monkey, *Ateles geoffroyi*
Starling, *Sturnus vulgaris*
Streaked Saltator, *Saltator albicollis*
Striped Kingfisher, *Halcyon chelicuti*
Summer Tanager, *Piranga rubra*
Swainson's Toucan, *Ramphastos swainsonii*

Tamandua, *Tamandua tetradactyla*
Tapir, *Tapirus bairdi*
Tayra, *Tayra barbara*
Three-toed Sloth, *Bradypos tridactylus*
Tinamou, *Tinamus major*
Tree Hyrax, *Dendrohyrox arboreus*
Tree Swallow, *Iridoprocne bicolor*
Tropical Screech-Owl, *Otus choliba*
Turkey Vulture, *Cathartes aura*

Violaceous Trogon, *Trogan violaceus*
Vulture, *Cathartes aura*

Water-Shrew, *Neomys fodiens*
Waterthrush, *Seiurus noveboracensis*
Weasel, *Mustela frenata*
White-breasted Nuthatch, *Sitta carolinensis*
White-crowned Sparrow, *Zonotrichia leucophrys*
White-footed Mouse, *Peromyscus leucopus*
White Hawk, *Leucopternis ghiesbreghti*
White-tailed Trogon, *Trogon chionurus*

White-throated Sparrow, *Zonotrichia albicollis*
Willet, *Catoptrophorus semipalmatus*
Winter Wren, *Troglodytes troglodytes*
Worm-eating Warbler, *Helmitheros vermivorus*
Wood Duck, *Axi sponsa*
Woodland Jumping Mouse, *Napaeozapus insignis*
Woodland Kingfisher, *Halcyon senegalensis*
Woodrat, *Neotoma floridana*
Wood Thrush, *Hylocichla mustelina*
Woolly Bear Caterpillar, *Isia isabella*

Yellow-bellied Sapsucker, *Sphyrapicus varuis*
Yellow-green Vireo, *Vireo flavoviridis*
Yellow-rumped Warbler, *Dendroica coronata*
Yellow-tailed Oriole, *Icterus mesomelas*
Yellow-throat, *Geothlypis trichas*
Yellow-throated Warbler, *Dendroica dominica*
Yellow Warbler, *Dendroica petechia*